Angels of the Merkabah

Illuminating Sacred Inner Wisdom

"It is not because angels are holier than men or devils that makes them angels,

but because they do not expect holiness from one another, but from God only."

-William Blake

Printed in the United States of America

Cover Design by Barbara McCoy

Published by New Genesis Publishing

171 Utah Mtn. Rd

Waynesville, NC 28785

Angels of the Merkabah by Bodie McCoy

ISBN: 978-0-9797493-5-3

Contents

INTRODUCTION

For the first time ever, we have begun an utterly new human story. The original story, called "Genesis," is about God birthing His Creation. Our new story is a New Genesis about us birthing our Creator. The old *Genesis* was a story of division: *"In the beginning God created the Heavens and the Earth…. and God divided the light from the darkness…. And God divided the waters…. He said let dry land appear… And God divided the day from the night…. Then the Gods of Eden divided Eve from Adam, Caine slew Able*, and we have been fighting and dividing ever since.

Historically we've justified the wars that divide us with lies that divide us more. We say we fight for peace and justice, but deep down we know that is a lie. We fight to avoid facing our own responsibilities. We divide and separate for the convenience of blame. With different countries and languages, we worship different gods, practice different religions and politics. We favor male over female and children over adults and vice versa. We root for "good guys" and boo "bad guys." And we fight to be *"right"* or at least not to be wrong. We divide and conquer ourselves until we let go to think, feel, and create as God designed us to.

As we ask meaningful questions like "Who am I", *"What do I want,"* and *"What can I do,"* we face our collective illusion of, *"After all, I'm just one person."* *Angels of the Merkabah* replace the illusion of separation that makes us all feel alone, with the loving awareness of our connection to everyone and everything. In the first part of our New Genesis story, *"We are a family of creators,"* still programed to perpetuate our Old Genesis ways of thinking. As our New Genesis story begins a new appreciation of our unique inner treasures unfolds, which have been repressed in the Old Genesis story.

In our New Genesis story, we will utilize our Creator's *Law of the Universe*, in new ways. But first we must accept that *"We can't solve our problems with the same thinking with which we created them."* The solutions we need now require each of us to accept creative responsibility for our lives. The old lies, like unity and peace are achieved with war and the *"King of the Mountain"* politics, must be replaced. In humanities new story we birth our Creator, who lovingly created us in her or his *"Image and likeness."* We birth our creator by letting go of all our programmed thinking. We naturally evolve this way when we are truly done and ready to begin anew.

Angels of the Merkabah have surfaced to guide us through the Pearly Gates of our *"New Genesis Heaven"* AKA New Jerusalem. They do this with spiritual exercises called Heart Dances™ that guides us to spin our Merkabah-Light-Bodies faster. Spin produces spiraling vortexes that penetrate our holographic illusions of separation. The special words and creative patterns that make these inner dances magical express the Truth of Unity in our heart's own feeling language. Heart Dance's magical words bridge, connect, unify, and activate our 4 light-bodies. And *"As we think, in our hearts (feelings) we shall become"* is the law that makes Heart Dances work.

At this moment most of us seem to fall into one of two categories: There are those who believe what is happening on Earth right now is just history repeating itself. At the same time others are seeing how very unusual things are. The world that invites us to exercise our free will is now demanding that we accept creative responsibility. Many are feeling trapped, wishing they could return to the "Good ole days" that they used to complain about. But something new and much better is emerging. We are waking up!

Our old ways of thinking and living were superficial and linear, but our new story is Holographic. These two views are opposites so, when you ask, *"What can I do?"* the answer is likely, *"Do the opposite."* In the old way of thinking we strove to improve ourselves and our world with control. In our new story we will change reality by *letting go*. In this new way of thinking we simply trust in the perfection of ourselves and in God.

The best way I know to introduce you to these angels and their Heart Dances is by sharing our own experiences of discovering them. I will begin with a story about the starship I created to travel holographically. We called her the LS5, our Light & Sound Synchronized Spiraling Star Ship.

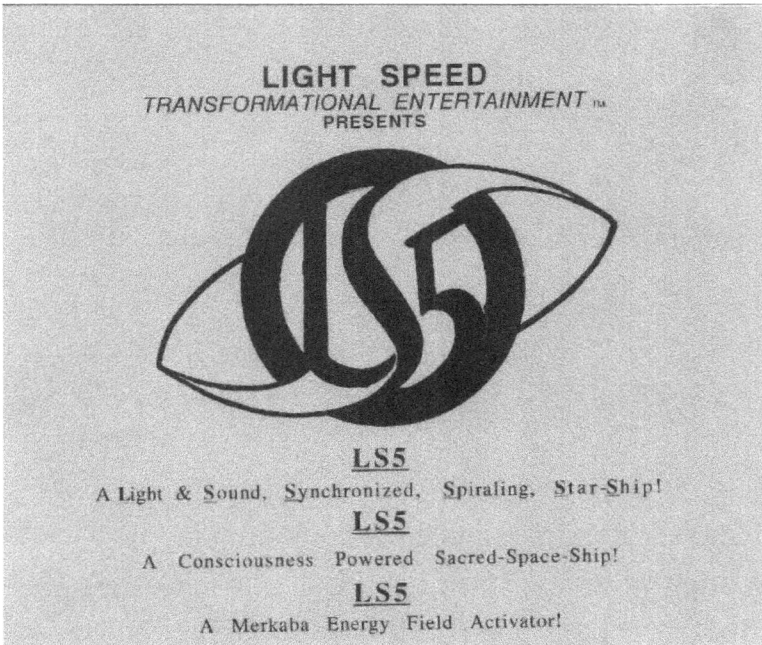

LIGHT SPEED
TRANSFORMATIONAL ENTERTAINMENT ™
PRESENTS

LS5
A Light & Sound, Synchronized, Spiraling, Star-Ship!
LS5
A Consciousness Powered Sacred-Space-Ship!
LS5
A Merkaba Energy Field Activator!

Part One: SPIRITUAL TECHNOLOGY

Angels of the Merkabah and their Heart Dances™ express a new way of thinking. Here in the following chapters of Part One, I share where this new way of thinking comes from and how my wife and I came to it. The most complete expression of this technology we know of is graphically portrayed in the Sun Cross Codex (below).

It is a detailed map in a two-dimensional form reflecting the holographic nature of consciousness and how to experience this holographic technology within yourself.

My friend Tom and I had just finished a fascinating conversation about holograms when Tom asked, *"Bodie do you know anything about UFOs? Do you know how they work?"* For over 14 years my wife Barbara and I had been discovering and experimenting with a holographic, spiritual technology know to *Jesus*, the *Mayan and Anastazi Ancient Ones* and the *Original Hindu Yogis*. We believe this technology enabled them to time travel and accomplish things that we consider miraculous. We had learned to use this inner technology ourselves to navigate past life regressions and construct meditations resulting in experiences of time-travel. We believe this technology links our collective Merkabah's, producing what some call *"UFOs."* So yes, I did have some thoughts about how UFO's work.

Tom was working with Doug Trumball the special effects wizard who worked on *"2001: a Space Odyssey, Close Encounters of the Third Kind, Star Trek: The Motion Picture, Blade Runner, The Tree of Life, Silent Running and Brainstorm*. Now Tom was assisting Doug with installing a holographic environment in the pyramidal Luxor Hotel in Las Vegas. But it was Doug's position as Special Effects VP for I-Max Theaters and his dream of creating realistic UFO experiences for I-Max that prompted Tom's question.

I told Tom how we had found the same spiritual technology embedded in the *Lord's Prayer,* the *Roots of Yoga,* and the *Sun Cross Codex* revealing a vastly different human story than we've been taught. I described how our experiments with friends and clients resulted in holographic time-travel and armed with my stories Tom got Doug excited about the possibilities. For a moment I even believed that Tom, Doug, Dan Winter, and I would collaborate to make Doug's dream a reality. But, after a few stimulating conversations with those guys Doug said the I-Max board would not greenlight our project and that was that.

Beautiful dreams can lead to painful disappointments, and I couldn't let go. So, I spent the next four months creating a portable UFO environment to engage our clients and students' creative imaginations. I built 12, 12-foot-tall towers with golden sunlike heads and cobalt blue faces radiating 474 rays of golden light each. Our center piece was adorned with 475 illuminated crystals, and we called her the *LS5.* She was our *"Light & Sound, Synchronized, Spiraling Star Ship."*

I hoped the LS5 would help merge our individual Merkabah's and generate sufficient energy to pierce the holographic fabric as we'd previously experienced in our meditations. We had often seen this spiritual technology that we'd first found in the Lord's Prayer dissolving rooms full of our students into golden light. We were hopeful the LS5 would take us to new heights, and for us it did, but not in the ways we'd hoped.

Her maiden flight had 33 passengers bathing in 6,000 rays of golden light from 12 light towers. Uplifting sounds flowed through 12 Bose speakers and her impressive looking control panel enabled me to adjust her lights and sounds. Everyone was fascinated but I believe the LS5 distracted us from going deep. And after three unsuccessful flights we retired her. I felt like I wasted 4 months and money we didn't have. As I questioned what went wrong, I kept

Figure 1: LS5 Control Board / Light Stand /And our dear friend Mary who has now passed over into the Light.

remembering how our 12-sun-faced light towers looked and felt like angels to me. We'd always wondered who was guiding our discovery of this spiritual technology and, as it turned out, creating the

13

LS5 was just another step towards answering that question.

As you will see there were lots of steps towards realizing how these Angels were the source of this technology. They had first appeared to us seven years earlier in what we thought was a *"message from space."*

That "message" led us to some new friends and to 7 Mayan temples in Mexico. All of these were steps toward consciously connecting with these angels. Now we believe those 7 temples were built with the same holographic technology that the 12 *"Angels of the Merkabah"* embody in us. In their Heart Dances we dance with these angels in our hearts.

In 1988 Barb and I were still discovering agreements between The *Lord's Prayer*, our *Chakras*, the *Original Roots of Yoga,* and some bedtime stories I created for our children. From these agreements, and the system of understanding they revealed, we decided to create a spiritual "game." But with no idea how it would work or what it would do, we weren't having much luck. Then one evening I was working in the Basketball amusement game on the Santa Monica Pier when I noticed how perfectly six quarters fit around one. Then I wondered what a gameboard made of circles would look like and that simple thought launched us into a new reality.

When the amusement games on the pier closed early that evening, I purchased 500 quarters. When I got home, I placed 42 quarters around a mixing bowl on our bedroom floor and laid 7 more rings around it. There were 294 quarters in all, and I learned that in Kabballah 294 is "*The number of Melchizedek*" to whom Abraham tithed. The bible also said Jesus was *"Ordained a priest forever after the Order of Melchizedek"* who was *"Without father or mother, without beginning of days or end of life."* I had

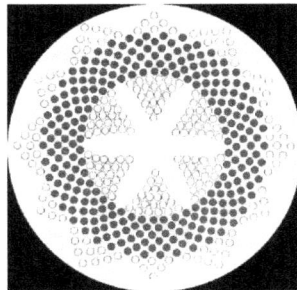

to wonder why I'd never heard the name *Melchizedek* mentioned in our church or catechism? Not even once!

To the 7 *"Rings of Melchizedek"* I added 12 outer and 6 inner points producing a 12-pointed star or sun with a *Flower of Life* center. That design contained 474 quarters, which Kaballah calls *"The Number of Daath"*. Daath, I discovered is the *"Invisible Seraph"* (shown as the white spere in this image) ascending the *Path of the High Priestess* in the Hebrew *Tree of Life. Daath* ascends through the void into *Kether* or *God Consciousness* through the *Unity of Opposites.*

Daath by Bodie McCoy

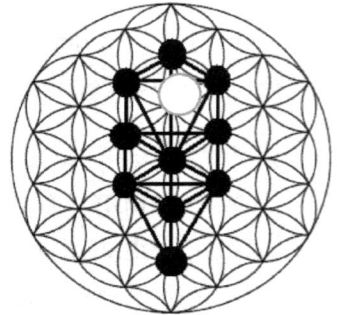

I'm not a graphic artist so there is no way I could create this *Daath* design consciously. It literally just came through me. While wondering where it came from, I heard a voice say, *"It looks like a message space."* Following that thought I went to a UFO symposium where I found people claiming to have been abducted by the "Grays." That didn't interest me, so I went to the Phoenix bookstore where I found

Carl Jung's book on "Flying Saucers." He concludes that *"Flying Saucers may be reflections of our souls"* and that rang true for me.

One evening while meditating on a crystal in our living room a small cobalt blue light, shaped like a flying saucer, appeared. What was that about and was it important? We didn't know what to think. The next day we visited our friends Ruben and Dawn and when Barb showed them the Daath design Ruben said, *"It looks like a message from space."* Obviously, something was happening and after a few questions Ruben and Dawn confessed to being fans of something called *"The Ashtar Command;"* a fifth dimensional group of etheric travelers committed to helping us through what the bible calls the *"Rapture."*

We have all seen Christian interpretations of the *Rapture* where the "good ones" are being swept up into the heavens while we rejects are left behind. The Rapture is mentioned in the bible 23 times. It's when, *"In the blink of an eye we will all be changed."* Thanks to the Hindu Kali Yuga and the Mayan Tzolkin we know it is not about who's been "good." It's about our current position in our galaxy. We've

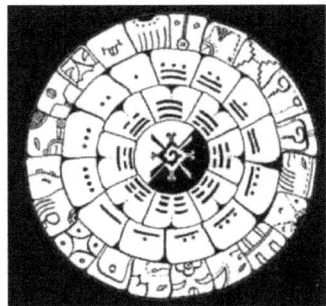

Mayan Tzolkin

just completed a 26,000 yearlong *Galactic Year* and have begun a *New Galactic Year*.

Tzolkin identified December 21st, 2012, as the day we left our Galaxy's Underworlds to begin this New Galactic Year. We are ascending into the Galactic Heavens just as the Bible predicts. Naturally, our fears of the unknown are being triggered as we have never done this before. Here in the Blink of God's Eye many of us are being changed by the realization that we are creating our own realities. Now we are seeing why it is so critical to be clear about what we value most.

Before leaving Ruben and Dawns' that day they lent us a small book called *"The Ashtar Command"* written by a woman named Tuella. She claimed to have channeled it directly from the Ashtar Command in the small town of Aztec NM where powerful vortexes, created by Anasazi Indians, gave her easier access to the 5th dimension. When Tuella's book left us wanting more, Ruben said he and Dawn attended weekly classes with a woman named Sai Vahini who also channeled the *Ashtar Command*.

Barb and I discovered that Sia Vahini's classes were co-facilitated with two equally extraordinary women. There was Sharula who said she was from the subterranean city of Telos founded by the survivors of Lemuria, and Atona, an angelic walk-in who said she'd swapped places with a woman named Diane. I couldn't tell if these women were nuts, impressive liars or telling the truth. But they knew things about Melchizedek, Daath and that cobalt blue flying-saucer, which they called the *"Merkabah."* The unusual beliefs of these three women seemed to give them extraordinary personal strengths and extrasensory abilities. We were and are grateful to each of them, as they helped us to find keys to open new doors within us.

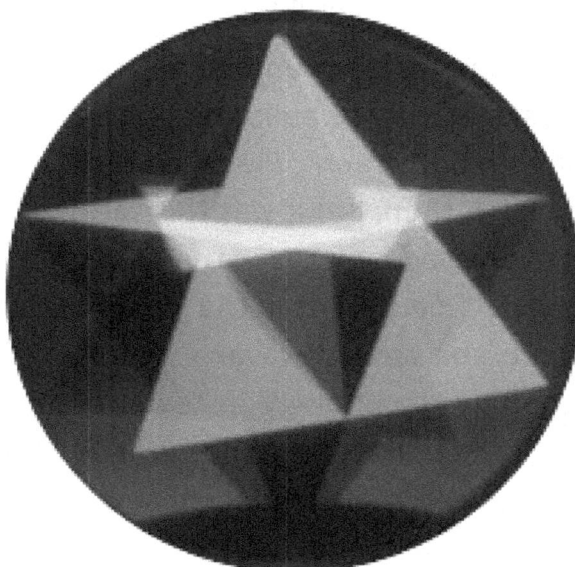

CHAPTER #3. THE ANCIENT ONES

The day after my 40th birthday Sai Vahni invited Barb and I to travel with her, Sharula, Atona and 100 others to seven Mayan cities in Yucatan. Just the night before Barbara had given me $1,700 for my birthday, which was the exact cost of that trip, so that was our sign. The trip's organizers, authors Jose Arguelles, Hunbatz Man, Barbara Hand Clow and composer/shaman Jim Berenholtz had chosen 7 Mayan temples to "*reactivate*" by performing the first large scale traditional ceremonies since they had been forbidden by the Jesuits 500 Years earlier.

For the next month as we prepared for this trip, we learned that slaves did not build the original Mayan culture, but with holographic Pleiadian technology. We didn't know it then, but it was this same technology expressed by Jesus in the *Lord's Prayer* and the Mayan Ancient Ones in the *Sun Cross Codex*. Like Christianity the *second* Mayan Culture misunderstood this technology. Instead of "*Sacrificing the Hardness of their Hearts*," as Jesus and the Ancient Ones taught, they sacrificed innocent souls to satiate their bloodthirsty "*gods*."

When the big day arrived, Mayan enthusiasts and spiritual activists from around the world gathered at LAX. From LA we flew to Mexico City, then to

Villahermosa and from there we bussed through the jungle all night to Palenque. Our first ceremony in Palenque was a Mayan baptism. Conches blew and

clouds of copal rose as 100 of us dressed in white, stood waste deep in the Usumacinta River. We lay back together submerging and emerging from the river's clear waters feeling renewed. It was the perfect beginning of our journey into the magical worlds of the *Mayan Ancient Ones*.

After our baptism I took a walk through the hotel grounds where I discovered a chained monkey that I had heard was quite friendly. I did not know there were two monkeys and this one bit my face! This caused concern amongst the many chiefs on that trip. Ego battels were common and yet they all seemed to agree I needed to go to the hospital for a "shot."

After standing my ground, just saying "no," Barb and I took another walk with Jim Berenholtz who we really liked. Jim said that many Indigenous people believe that when an animal bites you it empowers you with its medicine. He said that to the Mayas, Monkey was the "Trickster" much like how Native Americans see Coyote. He said, "Monkeys use pranks, stories, and

'Games' to teach us to think creatively and solve problems. Our days in Palenque were filled with ceremonies, meeting fascinating fellow travelers, and complaining about the "American" food served in our hotel. Our final ceremony in Palenque was a Peace

Ceremony facilitated by Jim Berenholtz at *Temple of the Sun.* As we walked slowly up the steps of that temple my heart filled with anticipation. I knew something was going to happen and as we stood before the Sun Cross Codex saying the Lord's Prayer Barb and I were both swept up into a vortex anchored there by the Ancient Ones.

In high states of awareness Barb and I both received visions. Barb saw herself as an eight-armed dancing goddess and I absorbed pulsing streams of golden musical notes, emanating from a sun, rising above a pyramid. It would be years before we would realize what our visions were telling us about our new game and the holographic spiritual technology that inspired it.

In Palenque we met a woman named Arleen who told us stories of the Anasazi who were the *"Ancient Ones"* of the *Ute, Navaho, Zuni,* and *Hopi* Nations. Like the

Mayan Ancient Ones the Anasazi were said to have been time-travelers from the 7-Heavens. Both Anastazi and Mayan Ancient Ones had

guided primitive villagers to create evolved cultures, and both were said to have come here to help with our current ascension into the 8th Heaven. And once their work here was done both Mayan and Anasazi Ancient Ones are said to have ascended, returning to their 7 Heavens.

These stories of the *Ancient Ones* are discounted as fictitious myths by historians and archeologists who still cannot explain their sudden appearance nor the mysterious disappearance of their thriving civilizations. While in Yucatan Barb and I chose to assume these stories were true and everything we experienced there seemed to confirm that the Mayas' Ancient Ones had abilities far superior to our own.

We returned from Mexico inspired by the belief that our world would change for the better once their technology was known and understood. Our 10 days in Mexico were so full that it took three more years and many difficult choices before we would appreciate how magical that trip really was.

We returned from the magical world of the Ancient One's feeling inspired. The fact that they did it all without wheels confirmed for us that their magical way of thinking was superior. While still in Mexico Barb and I sold our Venice Beach home, and two months later, at 3am we pulled into our new driveway in Durango Colorado with a *"Welcome McCoy Family"* banner across our new garage door. It was signed by all the kids in our new neighborhood, a stark contrast to Venice where we were robbed the day, we moved in. Durango Co, a small town in the 4-Corners contributed generously to *"The Game"*. It also provided a place where our kids could be kids much longer than they could have in LA.

In the 4-Corners Barb and I visited Anasazi Kivas with similar energies to those in the Maya's temples in Mexico. Kivas are circular Native American temples dug into the earth usually 8 to 12 feet across, but the

Great Kiva in Aztec NM is 50 feet across. It is one of 28 Great Kivas making Aztec one of the largest Anasazi ceremonial centers. Tribes from all over the Southwest would pilgrimage there to celebrate solstices, equinoxes, and holy days. In those 28 Great Kivas they

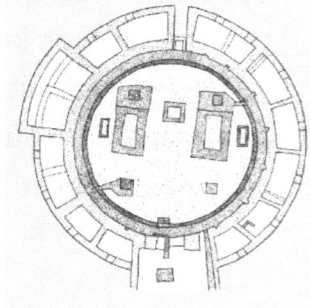

would have shared and participated in elaborate spiritual pageants and celebrations.

During my first meditation in the Great Kiva a female Ranger came in with a young girl and her parents. The Kiva's acoustics enabled me to hear her describing how shaman used the Kiva's 13 upper doorways to appear and disappear, mesmerizing and focusing the collective consciousness of their audiences. What I noticed first was how perfectly that kiva simulated an activated human Merkabah energy field and I imagined how it would have facilitated experiences of unity.

Then I heard the girl say she was seeing "*Indian Ghosts dancing in the kiva*." The ranger said she also saw them, and that they were nothing to be afraid of. "Kivas," she said, "*are safe places like Churches and their songs and dances are like our prayers*." Then I fell asleep and when I awoke, they were gone. I knew more had happened there than I realized but surviving in Durango and sharing our new "game" quickly consumed us.

In Durango, our "game" became popular, and we often heard our new friends and players saying, "*This is not a game! It's more like therapy*." "*The Game*" challenged its players to accept creative responsibility for their realities, which is a hard sell in a hyper-defensive world where the blame-game is so popular. In private one-on-one games (sessions) we visited past lives that exposed one's *"Original Sin."* Jesus expressed it from his cross saying, *"Father, Father why have you forsaken me?"* Deep down we all assume our Earthly lessons or "crosses" are punishment for something we cannot remember, and fear remembering. In Jesus's last words we hear him confirming that he too feared abandonment for being unworthy, just as we all do. But his final words, as he let go, were "It is done."

This "Original Sin" undermines our relationship with God and ourselves by denying God's Unconditionally Loving nature and ours. Original "sin" prevents us from fully knowing ourselves as *God's Children* and Him as our loving Father. The *"Game"* revealed vivid personal insights that made players feel exposed and those expecting to play a "fun" game often got extremely uncomfortable and some even got angry. The idea of picking up our *"cross,"* our *Original Sin* by letting it go, was the central message that was too holographic for the mind to grasp. To evolve "The Game, we had to learn to help players identify, face, and release their fears for themselves. Of course, we had to do the same ourselves.

We were finally settling into our new lives when our fears of lack compelled us to gamble our beautiful new home on a dusty old dream. It was a 50's Café with a jukebox, a dance floor, a soda fountain, and several cool pinball machines. It was beautiful but within a year we were forced to close, and our lawyer informed us we were too broke to even file bankruptcy. That Christmas our home with its beautiful views was facing foreclosure and our children's gifts came from some of the same Christians who had told them I was the devil. Regardless, I remember feeling grateful.

As Barb and I were licking our wounds and packing for parts unknown I finally took a good look at the *Sun Cross Codex* replica hanging on our living room wall. To my amazement it described our *'Game.'* We hadn't noticed this because the codex was so much more detailed and revealed

more intricate patterns offering clearer personal insights. That night the Sun Cross Codex blew our minds and opened our hearts, proving without a doubt that we had been entrusted with a truly precious gift. What we saw was the sameness within the Sun Cross Codex and our 'Game.' And from that sameness *"Oracle of the Heart"* was born.

A few days later our friend Mary, who'd recently moved from Durango to Atlanta Georgia, called to thank us. Our 'Game' had helped her through a recent divorce, and she was hoping that sharing the 'Game' with some old friends would help her reconnect with them. Mary set up a lecture tour for me and I spent three weeks that July touring the Southeast making new friends. And for the first time I made money sharing my 'game' that I now called *Oracle of the Heart*™. In Franklin NC I shared the *Oracle* with 40 of Mary's friends who gave me a standing ovation. That felt so good and so strangely unfamiliar. The bad boy was becoming the teacher while still unsure of what he was teaching. Best of all my trip to the Southeast answered the pressing question of where was our next home to be? After sharing The Oracle with a group in Waynesville NC, I took a walk in the moonlight and heard a voice in my head saying, "this is the healing ground."

Three weeks later Barb and I were packed and had paid cash for two U-Haul trucks, and seven nights in motel rooms for 12 people. But then our new realtor in Waynesville called to say the house we were planning to rent was no longer available. She suggested waiting a couple of months for the tourist season to end but that was not an option for us. Two days later, trusting that God was guiding our move, we left on what we chose to experience as our first family vacation. Yep, we were moving to Waynesville without a home to go to. Turning left on Highway 550 away from Durango I felt sad as our lives there had been rich with good friends, access to ancient Anasazi kivas, Colorado's amazing natural beauty, and powerful vortexes producing deep, insightful meditations.

To leave Durango we had to really let go, which was perfect. We had moved there in hopes of understanding our "game" better, which happened through our own experiences of letting go. Our ability to let go in, and of, Durango created a void sufficient to receive our true dream; to see 'Oracle of the Heart' blessing multitudes of people. We left Durango much lighter than when we had arrived, but we still had a couple thousand miles to go. On the way our caravan stopped at Graceland, the Grand Old Opry Hotel, and Nashville Zoo. The best part for me was hearing our kids laughing and splashing in the motel pools each morning.

On August 26, 1992, our homeless caravan arrived in Waynesville NC as the sun was setting. We had just enough money to live in motel rooms and eat at Denny's for two more weeks. Thankfully, the first thing the next morning our realtor's secretary saw a for-rent sign going up on the lawn of a beautiful old house in downtown Waynesville. It was larger, right in town, had a garage apartment I could use for my office to do *Oracle* sessions. And the rent was exactly half of the other house. Best of all: Mary's friends were already setting up work for me and *Oracle of the Heart*™ in Atlanta GA, Highlands, and Asheville NC. Our trust in God's guidance paid off. Phew!

Oracle of the Heart™ and I traveled five to six days a week until it became a demanding job. Simplifying the Oracle, so I could teach it to others, meant spending more time using it myself and less time traveling. We had learned a lot about our *Game* that became *Oracle of the Heart* from our players and students. Now it was time to use it for developing closer relationships with our own childlike hearts.

I noticed *Oracle of the Heart*™ pointing to my relationships with "secretive" people. I was amazed to see this pattern, which I was completely unaware of, woven through my most important relationships. The Oracle transported me to revisit an experience I had when I was 2 ½ with my mother. She had suddenly become depressed, and I was certain it was because of something I'd done. I felt desperate to make amends, but this was when mom realized she was pregnant again with my sister.

She had dropped out of school to have me, but mom planned to complete her college degree. She had to wait until I was old enough, and I had just started preschool. Mom's plan was on schedule until she got the happy news. So, I was part of her problem and the more I asked what I'd done the angrier she got. Finally, mom sent me to my room and yelled, "*Just wait until you grow up, then you'll see how hard it is*." That explained a lot; like why I'd been so eagerly take Peter Pan's Oath to "*Never grow up*." Just seeing how my irrational guilt over my mother's depression was playing out in my relationships was liberating.

This was an experience of letting go that changed my life dramatically. Some of those relationships faded and others got stronger as these insights changed me. Some were with clients, and some were hosting or promoting my work with the Oracle. And as I stopped feeling responsible for their pain, many of them lost interest. A handful of clients traveled to Waynesville for their Oracle sessions but that only lasted about a year.

As I pulled back, my dream started imploding. Both of our cars broke down and relationships cooled so again it was time to let go. It was during this period that Tom and I had our conversation that led to the LS5. In those days I was often reminded of the wise advice to "*Focus on what, not how*." "*How*" being the surprise that makes our lives magical. For some reason I kept thinking of my first experience in the Great Kiva in Aztec, so I returned there in a mediation. This time, I also saw the Anasazi Dancers and one of them guided me into their fire where I watched the Kiva dissolve. I saw a distant glimmer growing into a slowly turning golden cube that filled the void with a warm glow.

This vision was puzzling to me until a friend I shared it with said, *"It sounds like New Jerusalem."* When I asked what that was, she said, *"It's our spiritual destiny, where the Bible ends in Revelations. Saint John described it as The New Heaven; a giant golden cube with streets of crystalline gold, made of 12 precious gems, with 12 Pearl gates and **12 Angels** guarding them. In its center is the Tree of Life bearing 12 fruits and the throne of God. It's the inner heaven that Jesus says to 'seek within us."* All those 12s' made me think of the LS5's 12 light stands and their 12 radiant blue Daath faces.

As my friend spoke, I remembered the Bible and Sumerian tablets describing Eden as a Garden Paradise in the Tigress-Euphrates River Valley where the *Gods of Eden* are said to have genetically engineered our bodies and programed us to do their bidding. Then I

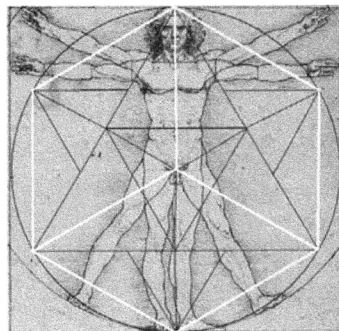

remembered a *"Flower of Life"* workshop where I learned how connecting a cube's eight conners differently produces an eight-pointed star tetrahedron, which is the form of our Merkabah light-bodies. So, we grow spiritually by shifting our perceptions and values from the outer dense, cube realities of our physical bodies to the inner spiritual light of our immortal child of God Souls.

Barb and I discovered this same star embedded within several diverse spiritual teachings and each of them identifies ways of spinning our Merkabah, star-light-bodies optimally. So, naturally I assumed there must be a connection between our Merkabah-Star-Light-bodies and the *"New Jerusalem."* This assumption proved to be fruitful. By focusing on this star or a teaching based on it, including Oracle of the Heart™, we convey to our subconscious heart that we are dedicated to Our Father's Will to *"Let there be Light."*

After sensing their connections to *Oracle of the Heart*™ I began visiting the Great Kiva and New Jerusalem frequently in meditations. Its 12 angels spoke to me through my own knowing. They said their jobs were to help us open the gates of 'New Jerusalem' the same way oysters make their pearls. By lovingly embracing the debris that finds its way through our defensive shells we transform that debris into empowering pearls of wisdom. Jesus described how we do this saying, *"to enter the kingdom of heaven you must sacrifice the hardness of your hearts."* This is also what we see in Pacal's and Chan Balum's sacrifices in the Codex.

Their sacrifices mimic the heart of the Lord's Prayer; *"Thy kingdom come; thy will be done, as in Heaven so also in Earth."* In the codex Pacal and Chan Balum are sacrificing the *"hardness of their hearts"* to Hunab Ku, *"God of the Central Sun."* Pacal's sacrifice resembles a beast symbolic of our fearful Idd and Chan Bahlum's sacrifice resembles a wolf symbolizing our controlling egos. Both are driven by fearful *fight or flight* instincts until we practice the spiritual art of letting go.

Jesus made his prayer for people whose hearts had been hardened by thousands of years of feudal wars and egomaniacal royals. Mayan Ancient Ones taught childlike hunters and gatherers who lived simply and naturally in small villages. From opposite ends

of the Earth the prayer and codex have united to help us see why we are and the geometries of light that empower us to create. The golden key to both the *Lord's Prayer* and the *Sun Cross Codex* is the *Unity of Opposites*. (Daath)

The prayer, the codex, the Roots of Yoga, the I-Ching, and Daath on the Path of the High Priestess all describe how the Light creates us to occupy the present. Again, this was the first thing Jesus taught. He said, *"Repent for the Kingdom of God is at hand"* so, *"Let go of the past and future as heaven is present. Stop looking for it over there, or there, or there because it's within you right now. Let go, be here how."*

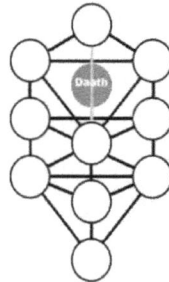

Awakenings occur as our values shift from outer material treasures to inner spiritual ones. Spirit is energy, and technology is a system of understanding. *Heart Dances* are systematic movements of the spiritual energies creating us and creating through us. Heart Dances mix opposed energies within us creating peace the way mixing hot and cold water creates warm water. Heart Dances retrain the mind to process life as it is, rather than as you think it should be.

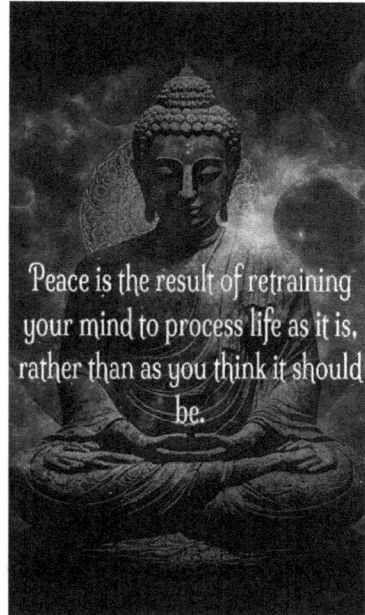

Peace is the result of retraining your mind to process life as it is, rather than as you think it should be.

The creative potential of this technology is revealed, in part, by the Ancient One's choice to create a vast civilization without wheels. Their own stories say they did this with otherworldly *"magic"* from the Pleaides. And their *Sun Cross Codex* offers a detailed view of how this *"magic"* works within us.

The Bible describes God as the *"All Consuming Flame."* In the Codex this *"Consuming Flame"* is Hunab Ku, and in the Daath Design it's a 12-pointed Star or Sun. We see this star reflecting the 12 Sun *"Signs"* of the zodiac, the 12 glyphs above Hunab Ku in the Codex, the New Jerusalem's 12 *Angels, 12 Pearly Gates, and 12 gemstones, the Tree of Life's 12 fruits* and Jesus' 12 apostles. We see all these 12's expressing the 12 inner qualities of our souls that these angels embody within us.

In Daath's 12 radiant outer points and Flower of Life center we see Heaven and Earth united in the light, *"As in Heaven, so also in Earth"*. Our unique positions in time and space produce our perceptions and our special ways of letting go to, *"Let there be Light."* We do this through the *"Unity of Opposites,"* which is also Daaths' meaning and what *Heart Dances do.* (Unify the opposites within us illuminating Litght)

Each of Daath's dots simultaneously participates in two opposed spirals, a large contracting circle, and a radiant line beautifully expressing unity through diversity. Daath's Yin, Yang symbol reminds us how the *Unity of Opposites* creates both balance and the lights

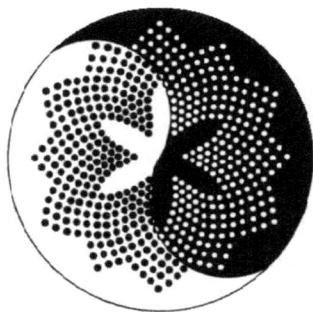

that spin our Merkabah-Light-Bodies, which produces the gravity that draws us into our Soul's Loving Awareness.

Daath's Flower of Life center led us to Sacred Geometry and the *Star-Tetrahedron*, which is the key to understanding this technology. This star is embedded in *Jesus' Prayer,* in the *Original Roots of Yoga, the Sun Cross Codex,* the *Tree of Life, in us* and every living thing.

Daath's Spider instructs us to let go, to be present, to feel, accept and learn from what our webs attract. *Angels of the Merkabah* guide us to hold better thoughts to create better feelings, to *spin* better webs and attract better lives. With *Heart Dances* we balance and cleanse our webs of defensive fears and beliefs. And the vacuums these dances create naturally attract our Highest Good.

Daath is humanities "*gameboard.*" Its symbols, patterns and numbers reveal the keys for winning at God's holographic *Game of Life*. The Daath Design speaks to our childlike hearts in its own feeling, geometric language. By focusing on Daath we bypass our controlling egos and thinking minds who do not speak this heartfelt language. Therefore, they can't distort its *messages*. *Heart Dances™* also do this.

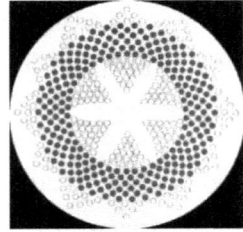

Modern scientists seek to understand the outer physical world to manipulate or control it. With this inner spiritual science, we seek to understand and cooperate with the creative energies within us. Physical technologies fail to deliver on their promises because they focus on Creation. Spiritual technology works by focusing on the Creator. Physical technologies have lots of steps that never truly deliver. With this spiritual technology we focus only on the goal, the feeling experiences that bring us peace and happiness.

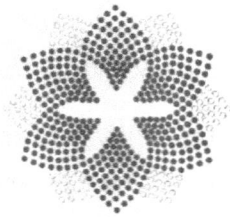

The rest just naturally unfolds from the blissful experiences this technology empowers us to create. Then it really doesn't matter where you are or who you are with. Because when you consciously create the experiences within you that you want, you produce a healthy detachment from the outer illusions, which is true "FREEDOM." And it is this freedom that brings you into the present moment, which is truly all that exists.

For years *Oracle of the Heart™* provided us with personal insights into how and why defensive choices follow us throughout life. It illuminates Karmic patterns, which contrary to popular belief, are not about punishment but are reminders. The Oracle reminds us that as the creators of our own realities we are responsible for every choice. It teaches how Responsibility = Empowerment = Freedom = Being True to our Selves. So, avoiding responsibility = avoiding creative freedom, perpetuating self-doubt, and limitation. We are born letting go, we die letting go, and everything in between is a lesson in letting go. *Oracle of the Heart™* identifies karmic patterns, and its Heart Dances help us assimilate the unlearned lessons in order to finally let go and experience true freedom.

Eventually we heard our visions at *Temple of the Sun* in Palenque speaking to us of Heart Dances. Like Barb's vision of the 8-armed-goddess, Heart Dances spin our chakras in harmony with the rhythms of our beating hearts and breathing lungs. These rhythms naturally dissolve our ego's controlling dominance with liberating experiences of blissful spiritual inner awareness.

Everything has its program, a tree is a tree, a tiger is a tiger and whale is a whale; only we have 'Free Will.' Negative thoughts and feelings cannot be positive, and positive ones can't be negative, but we can choose. It's when old fearful programs are triggered that Heart Dances really shine. The sacred essence of each word is an aspect of ourselves and by affirming them they produce blissful feelings and liberate us from the crippling illusion that the conditions of our lives dictate our feelings and experiences. That is an irrational belief.

Heart Dances replace our minds either-or, cause and effect thinking with magical thoughts. It doesn't matter if we make positive or negative choices as they attract each other. Whichever we choose, the other will eventually undermine our choice until we learn to dance with both equally. What we all want are the experiences of loving unity that come from the deepest letting go, where *"The Unity of Opposites"* creates Light!

There are 8 basic Heart Dances consisting of 4 opposed energies flowing through 2 opposed planes, forming 8 crosses and 8 tetrahedrons. Uniting these crossed energies liberates them the way uniting positive and negative currents liberates electricity. Heart Dances refocus our outer sensory awareness into inner Spiritual- Awareness producing experiences of *"Being in the World but not of it."* In Heart Dances we ride the *Law of Attraction* into loving holographic Soul-Awareness.

Our first three angel's Heart Dances balance our physical-light-body: the second three balance our emotional-light-body, the next three balance our mental-light-body and the final three balance our spiritual-light-body. In each Heart Dance the 1st step (or word) represents a Challenge. The 2nd step (word) represents an *Opportunity*. The 3rd is the *Theme,* and the 4th is the *"Ascendant"*. So, in our first Heart Dance, the *'Dance of Wanting,'* Receiving is the *Challenge*, *Giving* is the *Opportunity*, *Wanting* is the *Theme* and *Letting go* is the elevating *Ascendant*.

*First, we will share a very special Heart Dance, called the *"Dance of Ascension."* This inner dance is made of all 8 ascendants from each of the eight Heart Dances.

Science tells us that our universe is built on a foundation of interwoven waves of light and so is our own consciousness. Each of these eight words embody the highest expression of our divine light, which is why they make such valuable spiritual tools. If you simply observe how a candle flame freely and effortlessly releases its light or energy, you will receive some valuable insights into how your own spirit is doing the same thing in every moment. Like Our Creator, consuming is our nature, and these eight words will help you radiate your light, liberating you to consume your life more freely.

Move through each of the following steps breathing, affirming, and visualizing each ascendant as a flame within you. For your best results intend that this dance will heal our spiritual family by healing yourself. The more fully you feel each word and let it go to feel the next the more quickly and fully you will come to the heavenly present within you.

*Here we offer two ways of breathing this heartfelt inner dance.

- *Feel, breathe, and visualize each word or step:*

THE DANCE OF ASCENSION Part I

BASE/SEXUAL CHAKRA - I Am (breathing in), LETTING GO (out):

NAVEL CHAKRA - I Am (in breath) ACCEPTING (out)

SOLAR PLEXUS CHAKRA - I Am (in) APPRECIATING (out)

HEART CHAKRA - I Am (in) GRATEFUL (out)

THROAT CHAKRA - I Am (in) JOYFUL (out)

3rd EYE CHAKRA - I Am (in) PEACEFUL (out)

CROWN CHAKRA - I Am (in) FREE (out)

SPIRITUAL HEART- I Am (in) LOVING (out)

THE DANCE OF ASCENSION Part II

*Here is another way to breathe and experience this uplifting inner dance. Begin with I am – then say each word consecutively as one affirmation.

The Keys Within Our Chakras

I Am (breathing in),   [the Chakras they clear]

LETTING GO (out breath)   BASE CHAKRA

ACCEPTING (in breath)   NAVEL CHAKRA

APPRECIATING (out breath)   SOLAR PLEXUS

GRATEFUL (in breath)   HEART CHAKRA

JOYFUL (out breath)   THROAT CHAKRA

PEACEFUL (in breath)   3rd EYE CHAKRA

FREE (out breath)   CROWN CHAKRA

LOVING (in & out breath)   SPIRITUAL HEART

PART TWO: 12 ANGELS OF THE MERKABAH

Angels of the Merkabah speak to our deepest knowing reminding us of who we are and why we are here. Each Angel offers us opportunities to experience our creator selves with 'Heart Dances' as they unite our four light-bodies. Everything we offer about these angels, about the chakras they occupy, the prayer that expresses their purpose, the yoga that fulfills that purpose and all the rest are designed to connect us with their Heart Dances within us. Feel each dance energizing your chakras to spin your Merkabah-light-body. Answering each angel's questions and acknowledging how they make you feel will deepen your experience.

Each word of every Heart Dance is an aspect of you that exemplifies the sacredness of who you are and enables you to step into creator consciousness.

Heart Dances develop and strengthen us physically, emotionally, mentally, and spiritually. So, take your time and give yourself the gifts they offer from within to uplift you.

*Our first angel, the Angel of Desire, reminds us that *desire, or wanting,* motivates us to *give* and *receive* more. She asks us, *"What we want and why we want it?"*

*Our Survivor's fear of lack compels us to attach to what we want, which blocks our creative awareness and therefore prevents us from receiving it.

*Our inner creator embraces our wants as opportunities for letting go to create a void, to receive something better than we can imagine.

*The Angel of Wanting's CHAKRA is our BASE/SEXUAL CHAKRA.

*HER PRAYER is, *"And lead us not into temptation but deliver us from Evil (illusion)."*

*HER YOGA is *Tantra*, which her prayer beautifully describes.

*The steps of this Angels *HEART DANCE* are:

RECEIVING, GIVING, WANTING & LETTING GO

*Answer the following questions to feel this dance deeper. More important than your answer is how you feel about the question.

* THIS ANGEL'S CHALLENGE IS *RECEIVING*.

- How does *Receiving* challenge you?_____
  _____
  _____

- What do you like *Receiving*?_____
  _____
  _____

- What don't you like *Receiving*? _____
  _____
  _____

* THIS ANGEL'S OPPORTUNITY IS *GIVING*:

- How is *Giving* an Opportunity for you?_____
  _____
  _____

- What do you like *Giving*?_____
  _____
  _____

- What don't you like *Giving*?_____
  _____
  _____

* THIS ANGEL'S THEME IS *WANTING*:

- How is *Wanting* a Theme in your life?_____
  _____
  _____

- What do you *Want*?_____
  _____
  _____

- What don't you *Want*?_____
  _____
  _____

* THIS ANGEL'S ASCENDANT IS *LETTING GO*:

- How does *Letting go* lift or lighten you?_____
  _____
  _____

- What do you want to *Let go* of?_____
  _____
  _____

- What don't you want to *Let go* of?_____
  _____
  _____

The **DANCE OF WANTING**:

•

BASE CHAKRA: "I am *Receiving* (in), *Giving* (out), *Wanting* (in) & *Letting go* (out)"

Breathe & feel the *Dance of Wanting* 10 more times.

*The *Angel of Knowing* reminds us that Knowing is the sum of our experiences and intuitions.

*SURVIVORS experience knowing defensively as protection from the unknown. They rely on the discernment of others to avoid the responsibilities of Free Will.

*CREATORS experience Knowing as opportunities leap, explore, learn, and grow beyond their current knowing, eagerly learning their lessons of self-trust.

* The ANGEL of KNOWING'S CHAKRA is our NAVEL CHAKRA where our Karma gets digested. She guides us to use what we can and let the rest go.

*HER PRAYER is, "*And forgive us our trespasses as we forgive those who trespass against us.*" This angel reminds us that we are creators, so "*The forgiveness receive is equal to the forgiveness we give.*"

*HER YOGA is Jana, the Yoga of Discernment which her prayer describes.

THIS ANGEL'S HEART DANCE is the *Dance of Knowing* whose steps are;

DISCERNING, TRUSTING, KNOWING & ACCEPTING.

*These following questions will help you feel this dance deeper. More importantly is how you feel about the question.

* THIS ANGEL'S CHALLENGE IS *DISCERNING*:

- How does Discerning challenge you?_____
  _____
  _____

- What do you like *Discerning*?_____
  _____
  _____

- What don't you like *Discerning*? _____
  _____
  _____

* THIS ANGEL'S OPPORTUNITY IS *TRUSTING*:

- How does Trusting represent an opportunity to you?_____
  _____

- Who or what do you *Trust*?_____
  _____
  _____

- Who or what don't you *Trust*?_____
  _____
  _____

* THIS ANGEL'S THEME IS KNOWING:

- How is Knowing or not Knowing a Theme in your life?_____

_____

- What do you like *Knowing*?_____

_____

_____

- What don't you like Knowing?_____

_____

_____

* THIS ANGEL'S ASCENDANT IS ACCEPTING:

- How does Accepting lift or lighten you?_____

_____

_____

- What do you like Accepting?_____

_____

_____

- What don't you like Accepting?_____

_____

_____

The **DANCE OF KNOWING**

NAVEL CHAKRA: "I am *Discerning* (breathing in), *Trusting* (out), *Knowing* (in) & *Accepting* (out)"

Breathe & feel the *Dance of Wanting* 10 more times.

*The *Angel of Childhood* governs our physical light-bodies.

*She supports the Angels of *Wanting* and *Knowing* by honoring our *inner* child.

*Her child's perception is, "*I am*," which fearful Survivors interpret negatively as in: "*I am too small, too dumb, too weak….*"

* Loving creators perceive "*I am*" positively as in: "*I am good, I am growing, I am smart, I am getting stronger.*" She reminds us that "*I am*" forms the foundation of self-esteem, through which we see, interpret, and experience everything.

*HER CHAKRAS are our BASE & NAVEL CHAKRAS.

*HER PRAYERS are, "*And forgive us our trespasses as we forgive those who trespass against us*" & "*And lead us not into temptation but deliver us from Evil (illusion).*"

*HER YOGAS are Tantra and Jana, which her prayers beautifully describe."

THIS ANGEL'S HEART DANCE is the *Dance of Childhood* whose steps are:

"I AM LETTING GO, I AM ACCEPTING & I AM

*These following questions will help you feel this dance deeper. More important than your answer is how you feel about the question.

* THIS ANGEL'S CHALLENGE is LETTING GO:

- How does Letting Go challenge you?_____
  _____
  _____

- What do you like Letting go of?_____
  _____
  _____

- What don't you like to Let go? _____
  _____
  _____

* THIS ANGEL'S OPPORTUNITY is ACCEPTING:

- How does Accepting represent an Opportunity to you?_____
  _____

- What do you like Accepting?_____
  _____
  _____

- What don't you like Accepting?_____
  _____
  _____

* THIS ANGEL'S THEME is CHILDHOOD:

- How is Childhood a Theme in your life?_____
  _____
  _____

- What are your positive experiences of
  Childhood?_____
  _____

- What are your negative experiences of
  Childhood?_____
  _____

* THIS ANGEL'S ASCENDANT is *"I AM"*:

- Use "I am" in an uplifting statement about
  yourself:_____
  _____

- What are your positive "I am" beliefs?_____
  _____
  _____

- What are your negative "I am" beliefs?_____
  _____
  _____

The Dance of Childhood or The Grail

BASE & NAVEL CHAKRAS: "I am (in breath) *Letting go* (out), I am Accepting (in), I am (out)" (repeat 10 times)

*The Angel of Responding guides us to respond to all our feelings, both positive and negative, with appreciation.

*SURVIVORS defensively attach to feelings they like and resist those they don't like. She reminds us energy must flow, and it always will so let it go.

*CREATORS trust both Happy and Unhappy feelings to guide them to Love.

*HER CHAKRA is our SOLAR PLEXUS CHAKRA or "*Breadbasket*."

*HER PRAYER is, "*Give us this day, our daily bread*."

*HER YOGA is *Karma Yoga*, which her prayer describes.

THIS ANGEL'S HEART DANCE is the *Dance of Responding*, whose steps are:

UNHAPPY, HAPPY, RESPONDING & APPRECIATING:

NOTE: If you find the word "*Unhappy*" challenging observe how *Unhappiness* reveals *Happiness* the way a flame fills a dark room. *Unhappiness* prepares us to *Appreciate Happiness* and both *Happiness* and *Unhappiness* offer us valuable guidance.

*The following questions will help you feel her dance deeper.

* THIS ANGEL'S CHALLENGE IS UNHAPPY:

- How does feeling Unhappy challenge you?__
  _____
  _____

- What makes you feel Unhappy?_____
  _____
  _____

- What doesn't make you feel Unhappy? _____
  _____
  _____

*THIS ANGEL'S OPPORTUNITY is HAPPY:

- How is being Happy an Opportunity for you?
  _____
  _____

- What makes you feel Happy?_____
  _____
  _____

  What doesn't make you feel Happy?_____
  _____
  _____

* THIS ANGEL'S THEME IS RESPONDING:

- How is 'Responding' a Theme in your life?__

  _____

  _____

- How do you like Responding?_____

  _____

  _____

  How don't you like Responding?_____

  _____

  _____

*THIS ANGEL'S ASCENDANT IS APPRECIATING:

- How does Appreciating lift or lighten you?__

  _____

  _____

- What do you Appreciate?_____

  _____

  _____

- What don't you Appreciate?_____

  _____

  _____

THE DANCE OF RESPONDING

*Affirm to feel each step. _Breathe this dance 10 times:_

•

SOLAR PLEXUS CHAKRA: "I am _Unhappy_ (in), _Happy_ (out), _Responding_ (in) & _Appreciating_ (out)"

CHAPTER #12: THE ANGEL OF CARING

*The *Angel of Caring* reminds us that we care about what we are invested in.

*SURVIVORS who care for safety and comfort resist change by hardening their hearts to the pains of disappointment, which they believe are caused by Caring.

*CREATORS who care for Love open their hearts to Care and love wholeheartedly.

*HER CHAKRA is our HEART CHAKRA.

*HER PRAYER is, "*Thy kingdom come, thy will be done, as it is in Heaven so also in Earth.*"

*HER YOGA is Bhakti Yoga, *"Devotion to God's Will"* as her prayer describes.

THIS ANGEL'S HEART DANCE is the *Dance of Caring* whose steps are:

REPELLING, ATTRACTING, CARING, & GRATEFUL:

*The following questions will help you feel this dance deeper. More important than your answer is how you feel about the question.

*HER CHALLENGE is REPELLING.

- How does Repelling challenge you?_____
  _____
  _____

- What do you like Repelling?_____
  _____
  _____

  What don't you like Repelling? _____
  _____
  _____

*HER OPPORTUNITY is ATTRACTING.

- How is Attracting an opportunity for you?___
  _____
  _____

- What do you like Attracting?_____
  _____
  _____

- What don't you like Attracting?_____
  _____
  _____

*HER THEME is CARING.

- How is Caring a Theme in your life?_____
  _____
  _____

- What do you Care about?_____
  _____
  _____

- What don't you Care about?_____
  _____
  _____

*HER ASCENDENT is GRATEFUL.

- How does Gratitude lift or lighten you?_____
  _____
  _____

- What are you Grateful for?_____
  _____
  _____

- What would you like to feel Grateful for?___
  _____
  _____

THE DANCE OF CARING

- *Affirm to feel each step energizing & moving you to center by spinning your light-body faster, to shine your light more brightly. *Breathe this dance 10 times:*

•

HEART CHAKRA: "I am *Repelling* (in), *Attracting* (out), *Caring* (in) & *Grateful* (out)"

- NOTE: Observe how *Repelling* creates the space to *Attract* what you *Care* about most, even if you don't know what that is. Feel how *Caring* leads to *Gratitude* and *Gratitude* deepens your *Caring*.

"Repelling is a natural aspect of your light that repels what is not for your highest good.

By Bodie McCoy

*The Angel of Adulthood governs our emotional light-bodies through our Solar Plexus and Heart chakras.

*This angel supports the angels of Responding and Caring by honoring the Adult within us.

*SURVIVORS hear *"I am not,"* affirming their low self-esteem as in, *"I am not good enough," I am not able, I am not responsible."*

*CREATORS experience *"I am not"* challenging them to develop their unique gifts as in; *"I am not finished yet," "I am not as free or loving as I could be"* or *"I am not doing that again."*

*HER CHAKRAS are our SOLAR PLEXUS & HEART CHAKRAS

*HER PRAYERS are *"Give us this day our daily bread"* & *"Thy kingdom come, thy will be done, as in Heaven so also in Earth."*

*HER YOGAS are Karma & Bhakti Yoga, which her prayers describe.

THIS ANGEL'S HEART DANCE is the *Dance of Adulthood*. Its steps are:

I AM APPRECIATING, I AM GRATEFUL, & I AM NOT

*HER CHALLENGE is APPRECIATING.

- How does Appreciation challenge you?_____

  _____

  _____

- What do you Appreciate?_____

  _____

  _____

- What don't you Appreciate? _____

  _____

  _____

*HER OPPORTUNITY is GRATEFUL.

- How does being Grateful represent an
  Opportunity to you?_____

  _____

- What do you feel Grateful for?_____

  _____

  _____

- What would you like to feel Grateful for?___

  _____

  _____

*HER THEME is ADULTHOOD:

- How is the Theme of Adulthood effect your life?

  _____

  _____

- What are your positive experiences of Adulthood?_____

_____

- What are your negative experiences of Adulthood?_____

_____

*HER ASCENDANT is "I am not."

- How does "*I am not*" lift or lighten you?_____

_____

_____

- What are some positive "*I am not*" experiences?_____

_____

- What are some negative "*I am not*" experiences?_____

_____

THE **DANCE OF ADULTHOOD**

- *Affirm to feel each step energizing & moving you to center by spinning your light-body faster.
  - *Breathe with this dance 10 times:*

  •

"I am *Appreciating* (in), *I am Grateful* (out), *I am not* (in & out)":

*Observe how *Appreciating* leads to *Gratitude* and to being *Appreciated*. *"As you give so shall you receive."*

"What makes this challenging is the inherent sense of low self-esteem that an unconditionally loving, unlimited soul naturally experiences when it identifies with its limited, desire driven, sensory physical badge.

As long as you are here on earth you can't get away from these naturally conflicting co-existing agendas, but you can resolve them.

When you identify with your heavenly impersonal soul by encouraging your personal earthly self to "See Yourself Loving" then you are investing yourself in ways that will produce the conditions of appreciation and gratitude. Your divine inner child's innocence requires your earthly self to become a magical vessel or holy grail, to receive and overflow with your souls loving."

From published article in Spirit in the Smokies: By Bodie McCoy

*The Angel of Communing reveals how we *Listen* and *Speak*, to gain *Joyful* intimate *Communing*.

*SURVIVORS harden their hearts, which makes communing impossible.

*CREATORS open their hearts to make joyful communing natural and effortless.

*The Angel of Communing's CHAKRA is our THROAT CHAKRA.

*HER PRAYER is, *"Hallowed be thy name."*

*HER YOGA is Mantra Yoga, which her prayer beautifully describes.

THIS ANGEL'S HEART DANCE is the *Dance of Communing* whose steps are:

LISTENING, SPEAKING, COMMUNING & JOYFUL:

NOTE: Observe how you *Listen* to *Speak*, and *Speak* to *Commune,* to *Joyfully* touch and to be touched by a deep knowing of yourself and others.

*The following questions will help you feel this dance. More important than your answers are how you feel about the questions.

*HER CHALLENGE is LISTENING:

- How does Listening challenge you?_____

  _____

  _____

- What do you like Listening to?_____

  _____

  _____

- What don't you like Listening to? _____

  _____

  _____

*HER OPPORTUNITY is SPEAKING.

- How is Speaking an Opportunity for you?___

  _____

  _____

- How do you like Speaking?_____

  _____

  _____

  How don't you like Speaking?_____

  _____

  _____

*HER THEME is COMMUNING.

- How are communing, communicating and community themes in your life? _____

  _____

  _____

- How do you like Communing?_____

  _____

- What don't you like about Communing?____

  _____

  _____

*This Angel's ASCENDANT is JOYFUL.

- When has Joy lifted or lightened you?_____

  _____

- What brings you Joy?_____

  _____

- What deprives you of Joy?_____

  _____

  _____

THE DANCE OF COMMUNING

- "I am *Listening* (in), *Speaking* (out), *Communing* (in) & *Joyful* (out)":
  (Repeat 10 Times)

*The *Angel of Seeing* reveals how we see what we seek until we let go to see what is.

*SURVIVORS seek to find problems and danger in everything.

*CREATORS seek to find Love first within themselves, then within everything and everyone else.

*HER CHAKRA is our 3RD EYE CHAKRA.

*The Angel of Seeing's PRAYER is, "*In Heaven,*" "Within us."

*HER YOGA is Yantra Yoga, which is looking within the heavenly present.

THIS ANGEL'S HEART DANCE is the *Dance of Seeing* whose steps are:

NEGATING, AFFIRMING, SEEING & PEACEFUL:

*Observe how Negating (saying no) to what you don't want frees you to say yes to what you do want. And suspending both, Affirming and Negating, we see God's/Love's reality resulting in Peace.

*These next few questions will help you feel this dance. More important than your answers are how you feel about the questions.

* HER CHALLENGE is NEGATING (saying no).

- How does Negating (saying no) Challenge you

  _____

  _____

- What do you like Negating (saying no to)?___

  _____

  _____

  What don't you like Negating? _____

  _____

  _____

*HER OPPORTUNITY is AFFIRMING (saying yes).

- How does Affirming (saying yes) represent an Opportunity to you?_____

  _____

- What do you like Affirming (saying yes to)?__

  _____

  _____

- What don't you like Affirming?_____

  _____

  _____

*HER THEME is SEEING.

- How is seeing a theme in your life?_____

  _____

  _____

- What do you like Seeing?_____

  _____

  _____

- What don't you like Seeing?_____

  _____

  _____

*HER ASCENDANT is PEACEFUL:

- How does Peace lift and lighten you?_____

  _____

  _____

- What brings you Peace?_____

  _____

  _____

- What deprives you of Peace?_____

  _____

  _____

THE DANCE OF SEEING

•

3RD EYE CHAKRA: "I am *Negating* (in), *Affirming* (out), *Seeing* (in) & *Peaceful* (out)"

*The Angel of Elderhood governs our mental light-bodies through our Throat and 3rd Eye chakras.

*She supports the angels of Communing and Seeing by honoring the Elder within us.

*SURVIVORS experience the perception of Elderhood ("*They are*") defensively as in "*They are the problem,*" "*They are wrong,*" "They are unworthy" or "*They are too…...*"

*CREATORS experience "*They are*" as opportunities to serve, to share their gifts and utilize our Creator's *Law of Attraction* positively.

*The Angel of Elderhood's CHAKRAS are our THROAT and 3rd EYE CHAKRAS.

*HER PRAYERS are "*In Heaven*" & "*Holy is your name.*"

*HER YOGAS are Mantra & Yantra Yoga, which her prayers describe.

THE ANGEL OF ELDERHOOD'S HEART DANCE is the *Dance of ELDERHOOD* whose steps are:

"JOYFUL, PEACEFUL & THEY ARE."

*Observe how *Joy* and *Peace* enable you to give yourself lovingly in service to *them.*

*HER CHALLENGE is JOYFUL.

- How does Joy challenge you?_____
_____
_____

- What brings you Joy?_____
_____
_____

   What deprives you of Joy? _____
_____
_____

*HER OPPORTUNITY is PEACEFUL.

- How does Peaceful represent an opportunity to
  you?_____
_____

- What brings you Peace?_____
_____
_____

- What deprives you of Peace?_____
_____
_____

*HER THEME is ELDERHOOD.

- How is Elderhood a THEME in your life?____
_____
_____

- What are your special gifts?_____
  _____
  _____

- How do you share your gifts?_____
  _____
  _____

*HER ASCENDANT is "THEY ARE."

- How do you lift or lighten yourself by serving "Them"?_____
  _____

- Who are they?_____
  _____
  _____

- What do they need from you?_____
  _____
  _____

THE DANCE OF ELDERHOOD

*Affirm to feel each step energizing & moving you to center by spinning your light-body faster, to shine your light more brightly. *Breathe this dance 10 times:*

•

THROAT & 3ᴿᴰ CHAKRAS: "I am *Joyful* (out breath), I am *Peaceful* (in) & *"They are"* breathe (out & in)

*The *Angel of Accomplishing* reminds us that our *Accomplishments* reflect how we see and what we believe about ourselves.

*SURVIVORS see possessions and the approval of others as *Accomplishments*.

*CREATORS who know themselves as God's greatest *Accomplishment* know their Great *Accomplishment* is to *Love*.

*The Angel of Accomplishing's CHAKRA is our CROWN CHAKRA.

*HER PRAYER is, "Our Father."

*HER YOGA is Raja, the "Royal Yoga," to think and live as God's Royal Family.

THIS ANGEL'S HEART DANCE is the **Dance of Accomplishing** whose steps are:

CONTROLLING, LIBERATING, ACCOMPLISHING & FREE:

*Answer the following questions to help you feel this dance within you. More important than your answers are how you feel about the questions.

*HER CHALLENGE is CONTROLLING (focusing).

- How does Controlling or Focusing challenge you?_____
_____

- What do you like Controlling or focusing on?,
_____
_____

- What don't you like Controlling or focusing on?

_____
_____

*HER OPPORTUNITY is LIBERATING.

- How does Liberating represent an Opportunity to you?_____
_____

- What would you like to Liberate and from what?_____
_____

- Who or what don't you want to Liberate?___
_____
_____

*HER THEME is ACCOMPLISHING.

- How is Accomplishing a Theme in your life?_

    _____

    _____

    _____

- What do you like Accomplishing?_____

    _____

    _____

    What Accomplishments illude you?_____

    _____

    _____

*HER ASCENDANT is FREE.

- How does Freedom lift or lighten you?_____

    _____

    _____

- What does Freedom look like to you?_____

    _____

    _____

- What denies you Freedom?_____

    _____

    _____

    _____

    _____

THE DANCE OF ACCOMPLISHING

●

CROWN CHAKRA: "I am *Controlling* (in), *Liberating* (out), *Accomplishing* (in) & *Free* (out)"

Breathe this dance 10 times:

*Observe how *Controlling* (or focusing) *Liberates* *Accomplishing*, resulting in the *Freedom* to make our best choice to simply be present wherever we are.

"Accomplishing is our inner flame or spirit affirming its' true purpose and identity as God's accomplishment. It is being "The light of this world."

-Bodie McCoy

*The Angel of Awareness reminds us that our Awareness is the conduit through which Love flows manifesting and growing our choices.

*SURVIVOR'S awareness of problems attracts and perpetuates them.

*CREATORS who know themselves as God's Children know they want love and give freely of themselves to create or attract it.

*The Angel of Awareness' CHAKRA is our SPIRITUAL HEART CHAKRA.

*HER PRAYER is also, "Our Father."

*HER YOGA is Bhakti, the Yoga of Devotion to Our Father's Love.

THIS ANGEL'S HEART DANCE is the *Dance of Awareness*, whose steps are:

CONSUMING, CREATING, AWARE & LOVING

*Observe how you *Consume* to *Create* to be *Lovingly Aware*.

*Answer the following questions to help you feel this dance within you. More important than your answers are how you feel about the questions.

*HER CHALLENGE is CONSUMING.

- How does Consuming Challenge you?_____
  _____
  _____

- What do you like Consuming (taking in)?____
  _____
  _____

- What don't you like Consuming? _____
  _____
  _____

*HER OPPORTUNITY is CREATING.

- What are your Opportunities for Creating?__
  _____
  _____

- What would you like to Create?_____
  _____
  _____

- What don't you like Creating?_____
  _____
  _____

*HER THEME is AWARE.

- How is Awareness a Theme in your life?____
  _____
  _____

- What do you like being Aware of?_____

  _____

  _____

- What don't you like being Aware of?_____

  _____

  _____

*HER ASCENDENT is LOVING.

- How does Loving lift and lighten you?_____

  _____

  _____

- Who or what do you Love?_____

  _____

  _____

- What don't you Love?_____

  _____

  _____

THE DANCE OF AWARENESS

- *Affirm to feel each step energizing, moving you to center by spinning your light-body faster, to shine your light more brightly. *Breathe this dance 10 times:*

  •

SPIRITUAL HEART CHAKRA: "I am *Consuming* (in), *Creating* (out), *Aware* (in) & *Loving* (out & in)"

*The Angel of Mastery governs our Spiritual light-bodies through our Crown and Spiritual Heart chakras.

*This angel supports the angels of *Accomplishing* and *Awareness* by honoring the *Master* within us.

*Her perception of *Mastery* is, *"They are not,"* which SURVIVORS experience defensively as in, *"They are not worthy," "They are not good," "They are not me."*

*CREATORS see this Master's perception, *"They are not"* revealing the Truth of Unity: *"They are not because we are one."*

*The Angel of Mastery's CHAKRAS are our CROWN & SPIRITUAL HEART CHAKRAS

*HER PRAYERS are, *"Our Father"* & *"Our Father."*

*HER YOGAS are Raja and Bhakti Yoga, which Her prayers describe.

THIS ANGEL'S HEART DANCE is the **Dance of Mastery** whose steps are:

FREE, LOVING & "THEY ARE NOT"

*These following questions will help you feel this dance. More important than your answers are how you feel about the questions.

*HER CHALLENGE is FREE.

- How does Freedom challenge you?_____
  _____
  _____

- When do you feel Free?_____
  _____
  _____

- When don't you feel Free? _____
  _____
  _____

*HER OPPORTUNITY is LOVING:

- What are your Opportunities for Loving:____
  _____
  _____

- Who or what do you Love?_____
  _____
  _____

- Who or what don't you Love?_____
  _____
  _____

*HER THEME is MASTERY:

- How is the Theme of Mastery present in your life? What are you especially good at?_____
  _____

- What are your positive experiences of Mastery?

  _____

  _____

- What are your negative experiences of Mastery?_____

  _____

*HER ASCENDANT is "THEY ARE NOT"

- How does "They are not" lift or lighten you?

  _____

  _____

- How does "They are not" diminish Them?__

  _____

  _____

- Who are they/them?_____

  _____

THE DANCE OF MASTERY

- *Affirm to feel each step energizing, moving you to center by spinning your light-body faster, to shine your light more brightly. *Breathe this dance 10 times:*

  •

CROWN & SPIRITUAL HEART CHAKRAS: "I am (in) *Free* **(out),** *Loving* **(in),** *They are Not* **(out)":**
*Observe how freedom is giving to, and receiving from, Love.

PART THREE: INTRODUCTION TO YOUR STAIRWAY TO HEAVEN

Angels of the Merkabah embody new ways of seeing, responding to and thinking of reality. Historically we've engaged our lives negatively on all these levels; physically, emotionally, and mentally, which isn't bad or wrong but is incomplete. Life's spark is produced through the unity of positive heavenly, and negative earthly currents. Right now, we are suffering from too much negative physical, emotional, and mental energies and too little positive spiritual energies resulting in poverty, illness, and war.

Balance through loving unity is the gift these angel's Heart Dances offer. Each step is a special word spanning our spectrum of physical-emotional-mental-spiritual awareness. For example, you may easily experience Receiving, physically, emotionally, and mentally but our spiritual energies are elusive and more challenging to identify, to share with or prove to others. Spirit is fast and too fleeting to examine or possess in an ego-created world where possessions and proof inspire most of our choices. As spiritual energies are not valued or understood here, Angels of the Merkabah guide us to remedy this imbalance by exercising the forgotten spiritual Art of Letting go.

Traditionally we test the waters before engaging to feel, respond to, or live our lives, which is responsible for our snail-like evolution. It may even seem like we are moving backwards as we relive our lessons over and over. Now that illusions like time and space are compressing it is becoming increasingly crucial to center and occupy the present by letting go. God, who is Love, is always present, so Love's *Law of Attraction* naturally balances our unique imbalances as we let go. With thoughts of letting go we guide our hearts where they genuinely want to go. As you let go, you will come to the present where Love is. Angels of the Merkabah will teach you to be here and NOW, in Love, to experience and trust your best self and attract your best life.

In Part One these angels offered simple opportunities to experience how they affect our chakras. In Part Two we dove into the deeper inner workings of the heavens these angels occupy. Our goal is to begin opening the pearly gates of 8 of these heavens. As we shift to know these angels as higher dimensions of ourselves, we become more conscious of the potent creative choices they present. We will also use an ancient synchronistic process to identify which Heart Dance is attuned to our unique current experiences and challenges.

Now here in Part Three we will ascend through these heavens on an inner stairway. Ascending this stairway may feel more like riding an elevator. Each step is a pathway in and of itself extending like Jacobs Ladder between the Heavens and the Earth. The four steps through each heaven form a Heart Dance uniting the opposites of that level within us. Each dance liberates the energies of that level producing gently ascending vortexes, that gently lift our awareness. Like the angels that Jacob observed ascending and descending his ladder, Angels of the Merkabah teach us to do the same. The advantages and benefits of their dances are different for all of us as each dance guides us to the center of each of our own unique personal realities.

The Bible mentions of a type of angel found in the Merkabah called "Seraphim" angels. These angels appear like flashes of fire continuously ascending and descending.

CHAPTER #20: A STAIRWAY TO HEAVEN

By weaving the 7 Original Roots of Yoga into his prayer Jesus produced an incredibly special spiritual exercise, a *Master's Mantra*. This is how I experience Heart Dances as unique expressions of Mantra Yoga. Mantras are words often described as "Sacred Utterances" as they are used to call forth God's presence from within us. Heart Dances do the same but quite uniquely. Yogis say that mantras vibrate or resonate with the "Sound Current" that flows from God's heart to ours. Heart Dances also do this with the feeling energies they express.

Here we will emphasize how the 8 basic Heart Dances express an inner stairway resembling "Jacob's Ladder", bridging the heavenly and Earthly realms within us. The "angels" Jacob saw ascending and descending his "ladder" were the *Angels of the Merkabah*. They teach us to fulfill our purpose to unite the opposites of Heaven and Earth within us. The best way to know how this stairway, or ladder is within you, is to experience it. Please understand this experience begins in our mind and then our heart, "as you think, in your heart you shall become," our feelings will follow. Therefore, the importance of filling your mind with heavenly thoughts. And like any exercise, to experience these results we must persist.

We will begin here with two simple exercises, one to ascend and the other to descend this stairway. Please take your time and persist to feel how this divine structure in you. Also please know that what we experience as a lifting of our is also a progression of degrees of being present.

ASCENDING YOUR INNER STAIRWAY

Breathe to feel each step then move to the next step and the next chakra.

- BASE CHAKRA: I am *Receiving* (in), *Giving* (out), *Wanting* (in) & *Letting go* (out)
- NAVEL CHAKRA: I am *Discerning* (in), *Trusting* (out), *Knowing* (in) & *Accepting* (out)
- SOLAR PLEXUS: I am *Unhappy* (in), *Happy* (out), *Responding* (in) & *Appreciating* (out)
- HEART CHAKRA: I am *Repelling* (in), *Attracting* (out), *Caring* (in) & *Grateful* (out)
- THROAT CHAKRA: I am *Listening* (in), *Speaking* (out), *Communing* (in), & *Joyful* (out)
- 3RD EYE CHAKRA: I am *Negating* (in), *Affirming* (out), *Seeing* (in) & *Peaceful* (out)
- CROWN CHAKRA: I am *Controlling* (in), *Liberating* (out), *Accomplishing* (in) & *Free* (out)
- SPIRITUAL HEART: I am *Consuming* (in), *Creating* (out), *Aware* (in) & *Loving* (out)

Here we will descend this same inner stairway from our Base Chakra to our Spiritual Heart:>>>>>>

DESCENDING YOUR INNER STAIRWAY

Breathe to feel each step before moving to the next step and its chakra.

- SPIRITUAL HEART: I am *Consuming* (in), *Creating* (out), *Aware* (in) & *Loving* (out)
- CROWN CHAKRA: I am *Controlling* (in), *Liberating* (out), *Accomplishing* (in) & *Free* (out)
- 3RD EYE CHAKRA: I am *Negating* (in), *Affirming* (out), *Seeing* (in) & *Peaceful* (out)
  THROAT CHAKRA: I am *Listening* (in), *Speaking* (out), *Communing* (in), & *Joyful*
- HEART CHAKRA: I am *Repelling* (in), *Attracting* (out), Car*ing* (in) & *Grateful* (out)
- SOLAR PLEXUS: I am *Unhappy* (in), *Happy* (out), *Responding* (in) & *Appreciating* (out)
- NAVEL CHAKRA: I am *Discerning* (in), *Trusting* (out), *Knowing* (in) & *Accepting* (out)
- BASE CHAKRA: I am *Receiving* (in), *Giving* (out), *Wanting* (in) & *Letting go* (out)
  Memorizing these 32 words or steps integrates this Master's Mantra as your own. Levels are color coded, and each level has its own 4-word Heart Dance.

| Level 1. Base Chakra is Red |
| Level 2. Navel Chakra in Orange |
| Level 3. Solar Plexus in Yellow |
| Level 4. Heart Chakra is Green |
| Level 5. Throat Chakra is Blue |
| Level 6. Third Eye is Indigo |
| Level 7. Crown Chakra is Violet |
| Level 8. Spiritual Heart is Pink |

I AM:

1. Receiving	Giving	Wanting &	Letting go
2. Discerning	Trusting	Knowing &	Accepting
3. Unhappy	Happy	Responding	Appreciating
4. Repelling	Attracting	Caring	Grateful
5. Listening	Speaking	Communing	Joyful
6. Negating	Affirming	Seeing	Peaceful
7. Controlling	Liberating	Accomplishing	Free
8. Consuming	Creating	Aware	Loving

The Second Heaven's gate is our Navel Chakra whose angels are those of Knowing and Childhood. The yoga here is Jana, which the prayer, *"And forgive us our trespasses (errors) as we forgive those who trespass against us"* describes. Jana is the Yoga of Discernment and Knowing, which the Dance of Knowing expresses. Its steps are, *"I am Receiving (in), Giving (out), Wanting (in), & I am Letting go (out)*. To experience this dance, feel its steps in your breathing. Feel your naturally discerning nature being strengthening as you breathe and feel, "I am *Discerning*, *Trusting*, *Knowing* and *Accepting."* Feel how your preferences for one step over another imbalances and interferes with your Navel-chakra's energy system and how this Heart Dance balances your relationships with these energies.

DISCERNING: Each time we truly let go we enter a new reality that offers us new choices requiring us to Discern which is best. Like surfing newness requires us to discern, to position ourselves to ride new waves. Like a newborn infant moving from her mother's womb to her breast, we all have the innate ability to move on. Change, life's only constant, invites us to discern new ways of being in relationship with everything and everyone beginning with our own selves.

A fearful survivor's approach makes discerning new choices difficult. Our ego built Might Makes Right world also makes discerning and choosing difficult. Discerning to make new choices exposes us to criticism, failures, and the judgements of others. Rather than suffering their scrutiny or their own disappointments survivors follow the leadership of "experts" and "authorities" who our Might Makes Right world approves. While these "experts" eagerly promise to assume our responsibilities, all they are interested in is the power and money that we pay for their empty promises.

It's important to see how our world strips away our 'Sovern Responsibilities' and opportunities to love ourselves. As a result, we endure a pervasive, seemingly innate sense of powerlessness and hopelessness. That's a huge lie, we're all capable of so much more than being dependent and subservient to the greedy experts of our 'Might makes Right' world leaders. It's our dependance on their lies that makes us feel vulnerable, unworthy, and easy to control. So, the personal challenges, growth opportunities and creative empowerment that come with thinking and choosing for ourselves requires both courage and faith in ourselves. Like all strengths these two are developed through our acceptance of the creative responsibilities that come with making our own choices. This threatens their authority over us, and therefore they are amping up their fear tactics desperately attempting to put us back in our places.

TRUSTING: Trusting balances Discerning by raising the important question, "*who can I trust*"? The answer is, "trust only yourself" then you will learn the most valuable truths of all, the truth of who you are, what makes you special and what you need to fulfill your unique purpose. Only by trusting in ourselves can we discern who or what is trustworthy. Whether we trust their discernment or not it's discernment that enables us to engage with our own lives. Most of us don't even see the world we live in because we are so busy working to pay others, to manage our lives for us.

Health and politics affect all of us profoundly yet most of us know little about either. We trust those who claim to know, the smart ones who ensure that if things go badly, we pay the price, and they get paid. We trust them to play the Blame Game, which seems safer than accepting our own creative responsibilities. Once we realize how they've rigged the game we also begin seeing how it's the most irresponsible approach to responsibility imaginable.

We all trust in many things, some appropriate and some not. Trust is so important that without it we could do nothing and with it we can do anything. Trust is how we invest in ourselves by testing to experience the consequences of our choices and discernment. Survivors work hard to earn the trust of others, but they fail to trust in themselves. Like all personal strengths, we develop self-trust by exercising it by letting go. The precious freedom to be our true authentic selves is developed in Heart Dances.

Contrary to what most of us believe, it is trusting ourselves that attracts genuine trust from others. Faith is another word for the trust that our leaders, authorities, experts, organizations, and companies ask for. How many times and in how many ways have they betrayed your trust? Only when we trust ourselves can we know which promises are true and which are false.

Of the countless deceptions we encounter the most insidious are the self-betrayals we commit by trusting others more than we trust ourselves. The damaging results of embracing their lies and fictions is a world unconsciously starving for free will. Isolated from our true moral compass/hearts we give our trust inappropriately, in ways that erode our self-esteem. Searching for loopholes in God's Law of Attraction we waste our creative awareness ensuring our own powerlessness.

Like a good father God gives us what we need most, which is to discover our inner creator. This awareness of our creator-selves is what society's religions, law makers, doctors, bankers, and authorities all aim to steal. To know God's loving generosity, we must let go of our faith in the illusions of saviors and victims. We must think like his children, like gods and this is what Heart Dances will train you to do. Deep down we all want to know ourselves as gods because that is who we are. It is trusting in our unique goodness that enables us to think and live as creators, to see our needs as creative opportunities for letting go.

Letting go develops our trust in God's love through our individual experiences of his elegant, fair, and loving *Law of Attraction*. With persistence, practice, and a willingness to let go and receive we come to see how it is *"Better to Give (let go) than to Receive* (hold on)." In Heart Dances we give our precious trust to our own Selves, as God's children. Yes, we do have a lot to let go of and a lot to learn. That's why we are here learning to create ever more perfectly, and we've got a long way to go. It's time we stopped pretending to be an advanced civilization so we can begin learning from the advanced civilizations who have preceded us on Earth.

KNOWING: By trusting our own discerning, we receive permission to act and choose new experiences. The results of new experiences are new *Knowing*, new freedom, and new choices. Survivors who trust the discernment of leaders and experts forsake their opportunities to gain experience through their own choices. Instead of growing survivors erect walls knowing to feel safe and confident. They even shield themselves from the inconvenient truths that challenge them to experience more. They sacrifice their precious free will to feel superior by playing on someone else's winning team.

In the Second Heaven our Knowing grows as we release our fears of the unknown. By seeking comfort in outer fleeting illusions, we avoid knowing our creator-selves. Reactive survivors perpetuate their realities and feel that life is happening to them. Creators who think like survivors trap themselves within their own seeing is believing mindset. Round and round we go recreating our same realities lifetime after lifetime. To evolve beyond our current Might Makes Right illusion we must see to believe, to experience, know and create differently. This is what Heart Dances guide us to do.

ACCEPTING: Our egos avoid the unknown by compelling us to believe more than we know. Our survivor uses these assumptions to erect walls of judgment that isolate us by attracting the judgements of others. Our inner creator uses her knowing to liberate us from these karmic prisons into the unknown, to grow our realities by accepting more. Accepting is the 2nd Heaven's gateway to the present.

The 2nd Heaven's Yoga is Jana, the Yoga of discerning and trusting, to know and accept more. Jana Yoga resonates with our Navel-Chakra wherein we assimilate our daily bread or Karma. This heaven's dance is the *Dance of Knowing* ("*I am Discerning, Trusting, Knowing and Accepting*") mirrors the Dance of Wanting. We *receive Discerning*, *give Trusting*, *want* to *Know*, and *Let go* by *Accepting* more than we know.

The steps of Heart Dances flow from left to right then down and up into the next level. In Jana Yoga we *Discern* to *Trust, Trust to Know, Know to Accept* and *Accept* to *Discern, Trust, Know* and *Accept* more. The intent of Jana Yoga to balance and open our Navel Chakra is expressed by this heaven's prayer, ("*And forgive us our trespasses as we forgive those who trespass against*"). According to the Law *forgiving* ourselves and others enables us to *Accept* the blessings we've previously missed. This is difficult for survivors who choose to blame others for their problems and suffering.

Our survivor judges others to elevate himself. Judging others prevents us from learning from our own choices. Survivors who choose to "forgive" do so only to establish their moral superiority. With harsh judgement or harsh discerning, we spin reality negatively until it returns to us like a boomerang. By harshly judging others we assure that our challenges and suffering will be unending.

Creators experience Accepting as pure forgiveness. Survivors accept resentfully, or grudgingly, believing they have no choice. Like their lives they experience letting go as an act of desperation. To accept life's goodness, we must let go, we must surrender to its truth. A survivor's impure, conditional accepting and forgiving are just ways of holding on to illusions of control. By accepting and forgiving those who've wronged us we may see how our misplaced trust has empowered them. To embrace our purpose, to live as God's children, we must accept that every need we have is waiting to be filled, waiting for us to let go. The needs our survivor hides, the ones we don't want to acknowledge that empower us once we let them go.

As I began embracing this way of thinking, my life and especially my relationships changed quickly. Once I realized that letting go was Jesus' first and last teaching the rest made sense. When he said, "*The kingdom is at hand*," he was telling us to let go, to occupy the heavenly present. To love God, we must simply be present where he is loving us. The only thing we must give, to love God is Letting go to accept his loving presence by Accepting our own perfection. Accepting isn't the kind of surrender that our survivor imagines. In fact, it's liberating as all forms of letting go are.

The Angel of Childhood's presence here in the Second Heaven is expressed by the Dance of Knowing, *"I am Discerning (in breath), Trusting (out breath), Knowing (in),* and *Accepting (out).* These four steps play important roles in our later childhoods. When we are children, everything is new, so our young lives are about discerning what's what, who we can trust, what we need to know and accept. With discerning and trust we experiment to experience and know. Our childhood abilities to accept new things, new challenges and new points of view enable us to learn, grow and evolve rapidly.

"Science has proven that the results of any experiment are affected by the beliefs and goals of the one who is conducting the experiment. Your life is your own personal experiment, so it just makes sense to try proving what you really want to experience. To dance with God, we must accept His goodness unconditionally. Once we have let go, accepting is the next big step. The more we accept the more we can discern, trust, and know and accept."

Quote from Bodie McCoy from his book;

"Heart Dances."

(<u>Available in our Store</u> online at seeyourselfloving.com)

The Third Heaven's gate is our base chakra whose angels are the Angels of Responding and Adulthood. Its yoga is Karma Yoga, which is described by its prayer, *"Give us this day our daily bread."* The Heart Dance expressing this Yoga is the Dance of Responding whose steps are, *"I am Unhappy (in), Happy (out), Responding (in), & Appreciating (out).* We experience this inner dance by feeling its steps in our breathing. By feeling the empowering nature of *Unhappiness*, *Happiness*, *Responding* and *Appreciating.* Experience them unencumbered by any attachments, resistances or even preference.

The 3rd Heaven's gate is our Solar Plexus chakra whose angels are the Angels of Responding and Adulthood. This heaven's yoga is Karma Yoga, and its prayer is *"Give us this day our daily bread."* It's Heart Dance, the *Dance of Responding* consists of these four steps, 1.*"I am Unhappy (breathing in), 2. Happy (out), 3.Responding (in), & 4.Appreciating (out)".* We experience this inner dance by engaging its steps equally. Any preferences for one step over another will imbalance and interfere with our Solar Plexus-chakra's energy system and in this Heart Dance we balance by healing our relationships with these four inner steps.

UNHAPPY & HAPPY: Happiness and Unhappiness are like the two sides of a coin. We can't have one without the other. Unhappiness is the absence of Happiness which Happiness illuminates the way that light consumes darkness. We come to this world where darkness rules and true happiness is rare to learn what being *"The Light of the World"* means. For each of us it is as different as our needs are.

We've learned a lot about light's amazing worldly creative potential but truly little about how it empowers us spiritually. Our survivors have discovered many destructive ways of using light to destroy ourselves but have learned almost nothing about applying it creatively to our personal lives. This is an extremely dangerous situation as we have evolved weapons of mass destruction and if that isn't messed up enough, we have also not learned to make genuinely loving choices. Our destructive quest has polluted and poisoned our world. Though we know this we haven't the will to clean it up before we choke and starve ourselves to extinction.

We've done so much to make our lives easier, and more efficient, but have we made our lives better? Are we happier? I don't think so as Happiness is one of those things our survivor continues seeking in all the wrong places. What's the right place? One of them is our Unhappiness, which our egos compel us to avoid along all the beautiful insights into Happiness that unhappiness reveals. In many ways our experiences are like those of a greyhound chasing fake rabbits that we never catch.

Like dog and horse racetracks, our Might Makes Right games strongly favor their owners who for thousands of years have been manipulating our inner survivor's material values. They promote possessions as badges reflecting our worth, which makes controlling us so easy. Their powers of deception are so well honed just a few of them can control 8 billion of us. With promises of happiness, they've even compelled us to create a world where the things we need most are controlled by the relatively few "winners" of our Might Makes Right games.

Happy is getting what we want and unhappy is not getting what we want so those who control what we want, control us. We've built our top-heavy world on false promises of Happiness that distract us from our Unhappiness wherein the key to our true Happiness resides in us. The ways of letting go that Angels of the Merkabah teach are ways out of our historic material traps. Letting go centers us, spinning our Merkabah faster, by focusing the 32 lights/energies that create our Merkabah. Heart Dances guide us to surrender into our Soul-Center of Soul Awareness, which is the true fulcrum and source of our realities.

It seems incredible that simply affirming, with feeling, *"I am Unhappy, I am Happy, I am Responding, I am Accepting,"* could change us but it can. It's like a light switch. We don't need to understand how or why it works, only that it does, but only works when we flip the switch by doing the dance. If you say, *"I am Happy"* over and over with feeling you will begin feeling lighter and happier because it works. It's the spiritual principle that says, *"As we think, in our hearts (feelings) we shall become."* It's our feelings that attract or manifest our earthly realities. On the liberating wings of light and sound we convey our heart's intentions, which our Creator returns increased and perfected for our Highest Good.

RESPONDING: By reacting negatively, fearfully, to our own creations we perpetuate them. By responding positively, lovingly, and gratefully we make ourselves happier. *"Ask and you shall receive"* is the Law but when we ask for more than we've known life tests our readiness to receive. Not realizing how life tests us our survivor feels Unhappy. Feeling mad, sad, afraid, or guilty survivors give up before their new reality is delivered. Not understanding this, we often fear we are being punished when we are avoiding the lessons intended to prepare us. Instead of letting go we respond by hardening our hearts by blaming others for our unhappiness.

Creators respond to their failures and resulting unhappiness' as valuable resources of information. Things that make us unhappy say a lot about what is important to us. To a creator there's no more valuable resource than his pain. Unhappiness illuminates what we don't want, revealing through contrast what we do want, which is the most powerful information that a creator can possess. While survivors wallow in their fears of unworthiness creators hone their thoughts and feelings to attract what they want most. And there's always more.

Our Might Makes Right world compels us to resist Unhappiness as a weakness and attach to Happiness as a badge of success. So of course, fearful survivors resist Unhappiness by attaching to Happiness unbalancing the natural flow of our creative inner light. By holding on and resisting we   up stagnating lakes of negative feelings, which naturally attract negative experiences. With Heart Dances we erode our dams and drain our lakes of fears, hurt and guilt. What's left is love.

From dancing between Unhappiness and Happiness we learn what works and what doesn't work for us. In

Happiness, our hearts open saying "Yes" and in Unhappiness they close saying "No." By appreciating our happiness and unhappiness as equal blessings we see them as they are. They are our creative allies. It's like the ocean, life sends us waves of change, which we discern through our solar-plexus and navel chakras. It's seeing new possibilities on the horizon that enables us to choose, paddle and position ourselves, into our best rides.

Like newborn infants feeding for the first time from our mother's breast, we all must adapt. For fearful survivors making new choices to engage the unknown is difficult. With new choices we expose ourselves to criticism and failure. But rather than suffer the scrutiny of other survivors find "safety in numbers by following leaders, "experts," and "authorities." Those who are so eager to accept our responsibilities are interested in the powers ($) that come with our responsibilities. Angels of the Merkabah guide us to empower ourselves by accepting creative responsibility for our own special one-of-a-kind lives.

Where a survivor sees his responsibilities as burdens, a creator sees the *"Ability to respond"* as freedom. To experience our responsibilities in this empowering way we begin by accepting responsibility for our creative thoughts and feelings. Responding responsibly is responding lovingly because love is what we want. We respond with love to reshape our survivors' thoughts and feelings into our creator's loving instruments. As creators we give our survivor's fearful thoughts, feelings new meanings as we do in Heart Dances.

Our top-heavy ego/leader driven world needs lots of followers. By accepting our responsibilities society fuels our innate feelings of powerlessness, hopelessness, and unworthiness. We give them our responsibilities and our power. By letting them manage our needs we give away our best opportunities to pray and let go. By depending on them we abandon our co-creative relationships with our Creator and become complicit in their heartless crimes.

We all have lots of thoughts, feelings, impulses, and desires. In this respect we are like radios picking up signals inspired by our future fears and past regrets. We also pick up signals from those who we share karma with. The consequences of these signals are determined by how we respond to them. New choices produce new experiences and new Knowing. In the Third Heaven we develop the freedom to evolve our Responding and therefore our experiences and our lives.

APPRECIATING: Happiness and Unhappiness create our primary "Yes & No" guidance system. Honoring our free will often looks like attaching to Happiness and resisting Unhappiness but that's not true. In fact, this is how we dishonor our freedom to choose by choosing to control our primary guidance system. There's just one way to benefit from this system and it isn't easy. To follow our heart's guidance, we must Appreciate our Happiness and Unhappiness equally, as valuable information about how to create our best lives. And that's our only purpose here.

We let go to accept and accept to appreciate. The more we let go the more we can accept something new or more, and the more we accept the more we can appreciate. As with all things, our outer experiences of appreciation reflect our appreciation of ourselves. Deep down we all know how this works, but survivors get it backwards. Thinking their value lies in the things they possess is the opposite of creators who know their value is determined by how much they can let go. The letting go that defines the Third Heaven is Appreciating, which is also how we come to the present here.

"Appreciating transforms our burden of responsibility into the ability to respond positively and creatively. Appreciating enables us to transform what we have into what we truly want. Appreciating can even help us to experience our deepest pain positively, and unhappiness may be experienced as blessed creative opportunities."

Quote by Bodie McCoy from his book 'Heart Dance" page 74.

The challenging changes we are experiencing are signs that our world is evolving. Our relationships with everything, especially with ourselves, are all changing. And most of us aren't responding with appreciation because we haven't even accepted the problems we have. Instead, we hold on tighter to our past and illusions of control. Yes, we have been doing this for generations, but this time the existence of our species depends on us letting go to accept and appreciate our new opportunities for healing, creating, and letting go.

We've never had more reasons to be Happy or Unhappy, or to Respond by Appreciating our opportunities to love God, ourselves, and one another. Our brilliant time is finally exposing our survivors' lies, which our current realities are built upon. It's our time to question where we are, who we are, who we've followed and why. Responding with appreciation to our world's reflections of our fragmented selves reveals healing opportunities to let go, accept, and appreciate our unique selves.

It's easy to appreciate what we enjoy or love but to appreciate things we hate, and resist requires new faith. The faith we need now develops from new life experiments. A survivor's life experiments aim to prove that human nature and life itself are negative and therefore must be controlled. A creator's experiments strive to reveal how life and human nature invite us to cooperate and co-create with life's goodness and our own. Recent experiments have revealed how our beliefs affect our experiments offering proof that regardless of what we believe we are creators.

Our experiments develop around assumptions that we either strive to prove or disprove. To grow we must believe in more than we know by assuming more than we know and testing our assumption. The magical reality is revealed when we assume what is true and the universe agrees with us as we agree with it. And of course, the opposite is true. When we assume what is not true, we experience the universe disagreeing with us because we agree with it. Universal agreement is the basis of true magic.

To a survivor magic is impossible as he is unable to see how he's created his reality. The way a survivor must see to believe he then recreates what he believes, blinding him to his higher creative nature. He keeps creating the same experiences in new ways creating illusions like being unlucky or cursed or having bad karma. Historically what we have called "progress" are more subtill, mental ways of hunting and gathering. What has not changed is how our thoughts, feelings, responses, and creations are still motivated by our survivor's fears. Our outer lives reflect our inner relationships with ourselves so, to make real progress we must shift from thinking as survivors to thinking as creators. It's our creator's thinking that moves us from reactive "*Seeing is Believing*" to creative "*Believing is Seeing*" realities.

It is believing in ourselves as creators that reveals our magical, holographic creator's abilities. If, "A picture is worth a thousand words" then an experience is worth a thousand pictures. So, our transition unfolds as we feel our Creator's light flowing through our awareness. By responding with appreciation to these inner lights we begin appreciating and responding to our fears as useful creative awareness. We "*love our enemies*" (our fears) as Christ did by appreciating the creative opportunities they offer as our allies.

The Third Heaven's Yoga, Karma Yoga, teaches us to consume our daily bread (lessons). Karma Yoga resonates with our Solar Plexus Chakra or "*Breadbasket*" into which we receive our daily bread. This heaven's dance is the *Dance of Responding* ("*Unhappy, Happy, Responding & Appreciating*"): From our Unhappiness and Happiness we learn what is truly important to us and how to create it. By Responding to and Appreciating Happiness and Unhappiness equally we make them our valuable creative allies.

In this Heart Dance as in Karma Yoga we consume our Daily Bread (our Happiness and Unhappiness) to digest the insights they offer. The intent of Karma Yoga and this dance is to access and refocus the powerfully creative emotional energies rooted in our Solar Plexus Chakra. This same intent is expressed by this heaven's prayer, ("*Give us this day our daily bread*"). In accord with the Law, ("*As you plant so shall you reap*"), Karma Yoga and the Dance of Responding guide us to evolve by responding as creators to our survivor's creations.

Imagine the CEO of a company is fired for not doing his job and you get promoted to clean up his mess.

The CEO is your survivalist ego whose false powers come from playing the *Blame Game,* masterfully. You are the creator who steps up to accept creative responsibility for his misguided creations by Appreciating them as the creative opportunities they truly. Our survivors are now behaving and creating more irresponsibly than ever. They think there is no way they can clean up the mess they've created, and they are right. Whatever was created with fear and blame challenges us now to affirm and exercise our creative freedom as God's children. As God's children we use our adult mind to liberate our inner child to create naturally by letting go.

The Angel of Adulthood's presence here is revealed in the Dance of Responding ("I am, Unhappy, Happy, Responding & Appreciating"). Consider how *Unhappy, Happy, Responding* and *Appreciating* play roles in our early adulthoods. Transitioning from childhood to adulthood is an emotional experience, which too few of us complete successfully. Sadly, our world does not value children so most of us lack the self-confidence needed to realize our special purpose as healthy adults embracing our challenges as valuable growth opportunities.

For children everything is new requiring them to discern whose who and what's what. But most of us enter adulthood with underdeveloped discernment. Having poor judgement, we are taken in by predatory liars, and codependent partners. Those who are fortunate enough to be appreciated as children are much more able to discern the higher guidance of their feelings of Happiness and Unhappiness. But no matter how fortunate we were as children our abilities to discern how we are creating our own unique realities is unlikely. In this world we all deal with our survivor's defensive feelings and instincts.

The 4th Heaven's gate is in our Heart Chakras whose angels are those of Caring and Adulthood. This heaven's yoga is Bhakti Yoga, the yoga of devotion, which this heaven's prayer, ("*Thy kingdom come thy will be done, as it is in Heaven so also in Earth*") beautifully expresses. To realize the purpose of Bhakti Yoga on this level we must be grateful for God's ever-present will, AKA *Love*.

This heaven's Heart Dance, the *Dance of Caring* is, "*I am Repelling (breathing in), Attracting (out), Caring (in), & Grateful (out).*" In this dance we devote ourselves to gratefully embracing God's loving will's presence in our lives. This is challenging as our survivor reacts defensively when he feels his will is being opposed as it often is. This inner dance will help you feel blessed even when you feel opposed because you are. God allows what some call the "Loyal Forces of Opposition" whose job is to test our readiness to make our shift from survivors to creators.

REPELLING: Repelling is the first step of this dance. Survivors who experience repelling as rejection don't like it at all. When something we want remains beyond our reach our survival instincts are triggered. This happens whenever something or someone we want or need seems unattainable. Repelling is our soul protecting us from things that would prevent or delay our awakening. To realize who we are we all need lots of experience and lessons in letting go and repelling is a primary way this is accomplished.

Our lives present us with many choices, some positive, some negative and *"one person's medicine is another's poison."* The globalist elites have done an impressive job of selling us on a one size fits all mentality. They've provided us with countless, meaningless choices and have convinced us it's freedom. The promise of gaining freedom by giving up our individuality has been swallowed by billions but not all. As clever and powerful as they are their plans go against nature, but the Truth rises like cream when we stop when we let go. As we realize the powerful wisdom of "less is more" we see their insane ego trips believing they can control and manipulate God and his nature by controlling our minds.

They might be insane, but the Elite know we are creators, co-creating Earth's realities with our Creator. The crazy part is that they believe they can control earth by controlling us and their plans seem to be working until now. Time is unfolding too quickly now for their sight of hand trickery. Through their efforts to strip away our uniqueness and remake us into more convenient, pliable humans, we have been subjected to sophisticated brainwashing techniques. We've been suckered and programed with TV, advertising, fictitious histories, material values, and other disenfranchising lies. While their efforts to control us do appear to be working many of us are also learning about who they are, who we are, what is important and what's really going on here.

Growing up in this world we naturally lack the self-esteem to follow our heart's guidance. A closing heart says, "*No that's not for us*" and an opening heart says, "*Yes this is what we need right now*." To follow our hearts, we must let what we think we know go to be present. Yesterday's yes might be today's no and vice versa but every day we are the creators of our own reality. So, every day it's our job to be present to know, make and attract our best choices and repel the rest.

ATTRACTING: Just as our Soul repels what is not our Highest Good it also attracts what is. But our blessings are often not what we think we want or need so each time we ask to attract something new we need to make room to receive it. Making room for something new or more often requires new wisdom and new strengths we need to manage them for our Highest Good.

The energies that protect us and attract our needs are the qualities of Love who produce the Creator's Law of Attraction. These energies that fill every need flow through our hearts and minds where they are shaped by our beliefs, which are shaped by the world we live in. It is our responsibility to change our fear-based controlling beliefs into love-based liberating ones. Foundational beliefs formed when we are children feel like parts of us so changing them often feels like self-betrayal. And the people who those beliefs have attracted into our lives may also feel betrayed.

Survivors who try to control or manipulate the Law of Attraction fail because that's not how it works. Our controlling minds are linear, and our hearts are holographic. Our job is to use our thinking minds to guide our feeling hearts back to their natural childlike programs by letting go. We do this by speaking our heart's feeling geometric language as we do in Heart Dances. These healing, feeling heart-songs express our heart's sacred creative purpose to attract our Highest Good.

To play an instrument well requires dedication and practice. This is especially true of our human instruments. And if we stop practicing, we slide back into our survivor's defensive ways of thinking, feeling, and attracting our fears and what we don't want. This old way of thinking is what we need to let go of in order to attract our heart's desires. Knowing ourselves as cocreators with God seems impossible until we recognize and experience the Law of Attraction responding to our thoughts and feelings.

CARING: Caring is the theme of our Heart Chakra, which is our creative center, the center of our bodies and the center of the Lord's Prayer. What we Care about we attract but few of us realize this as our survivor's fearful Caring dominates attracting things we don't want. And our reluctance to accept creative responsibility for our own suffering prevents us from letting go. Our survivor's Love of physical things and comfort prevents us from knowing our soul's caring for Love, which is our true purpose, our Highest Good and our true nature. The things our survivor holds are the things our creator lets go to create a space for Love to fill.

Our unique needs are the vacuums through which we experience Love differently. Here, in the *Fourth Heaven* we release our differences to realize our soul's universal Caring. Outwardly focused survivors care about physical things they can possess or accomplish until our failures compel us to follow "experts" and "leaders" whose greed, lies and lack of sincere caring lead to much suffering.

Believing we must beat those criminals at their own game is a huge waste because it doesn't work. It's their game and it's rigged with fancy words specifically designed to prevent us from understanding. Our creator is superior to their survivor whose fears are inferior to our Love. Survivors care about stuff and creators care about the energies of attraction. Our creator's creative freedom is superior to our survivor's desires to possess. So, armed with faith in our goodness, we claim the freedom to occupy the 8th Heaven of Unconditional Love within us.

By letting go we surrender to our highest caring, which attracts our Highest Good. A survivor wants proof before letting go of the outer things that he values above all. Letting is impossible until we honor our soul's caring, which requires faith in the goodness of everything. To believe in Love's unconditional goodness we must let go unconditionally.

Our values define our caring and our caring defines our values, which define how Love flows creating our realities. Realizing how our Creator's Love flows through our caring and values empowers us to reshape our realities by reshaping our values and caring. In Heart Dances we align with our soul's caring, agreeing with the universal plan, so the universe agrees with us. By affirming the energies with which we are created, as we do in Heart Dances, we evolve our naturally co-creative relationships with the whole universe.

In Heart Dances we ride these pure creative energies to their Source within us and according to the law they return to us bearing gifts. The heart-felt lights of Caring flowing through us often attract our Highest Good in forms we think we don't want. Our survivor's defensive caring attracts fears for our Highest Good. Caring for Love more than our fears reveals them as opportunities to love. Accepting our fears as blessings liberates us to live and love unconditionally.

GRATEFUL: We open our hearts to care unconditionally with unconditional Gratitude. That means absolutely everything. If that sounds impossible, it is, but it's also the only way to freedom. So, "Fake it, till you make it" is the way. Even if you attract something you neither want, nor need, say "thank you." If you don't feel it that's ok, there's a blessing in everything. By using gratitude for everything and everyone changes challenges into opportunities. And the way God's children awaken is by trusting that He is always and everywhere lovingly unfolding what is for our Highest Good.

Feeling Grateful is often the gift we give ourselves for honoring our soul's deepest caring. Even when we aren't clear what it is. Our survivors defensively harden our hearts to anything they can't control, so being grateful for invisible blessings isn't in their range. When our senses collude with the world placing things like money, comforts, and privileges in our way we undermine our own integrity. Assigning false values and meaning to things like cars, gems, credentials, and mansions just constructs endless self-sabotaging illusions.

Our reward for achieving our lofty material goals is to realize they are false and illusionary. Goals to possess the clearest diamonds, the biggest mansions, the fastest cars, and the most luxurious yachts are all false forms of satisfaction and can never make us genuinely happy or feel successful. Because we are creators our beliefs in these illusions do produce temporary happy feelings blinding us to the air, food, and water they pollute and destroy. And our survivors' controlling efforts to clean up the mess only make it worse. It's absurd to think that we can solve our problems with the same thinking that created them.

Grateful is the highest dimension of our Physical and Emotional Light bodies and Loving is our Mental and Spiritual Light body's highest dimension. *'Gratitude'* occupies our emotional hearts and *'Loving'* occupies our spiritual hearts. Gratitude is the gateway that opens our hearts to Loving. People say they want to please God, but He is always pleased. The idea that the Creator's moods rise and fall because of us is a testimony to our ego's hubris. As God's Children we have just one challenge; to be grateful for every breath, each and each moment that follows. All of it!

Like a trampoline, Gratitude launches us from our survivor consciousness into our creator consciousness. Unconditional gratitude moves us from a self-perpetuating *"Seeing is Believing"* limited reality to a self-fulfilling *"Believing is Seeing"* creative platform. Our snail-like evolution is largely a result of us seeing and reacting defensively to our own creations. By practicing faith in God's goodness and ours we empower our inner creator to manifest what is for our Highest Good consciously.

The Forth Heaven's Bhakti Yoga is the Yoga of devotion to God's ever-present power and goodness. Bhakti resonates with both our Heart Chakras. This heaven's dance is the *Dance of Caring*: *"Repelling, Attracting, Caring & Grateful."* By observing our experiences of Repelling and Attracting we learn a lot about how the Law of Attraction responds to our unique Caring and for these insights we can be Grateful. By Appreciating our experiences of Repelling and Attracting equally we evolve from survivor to creator consciousness rapidly.

In this Heart Dance as in Bhakti Yoga we honor the loving power and will of our Creator by assuming His/Her will (love) is always being done, which is expressed in the Lord's Prayer's Heart Chakra attunement, (*"Thy kingdom come, thy will be done as it is in Heaven so also in Earth"*). Bhakti Yoga, like the Dance of Caring focuses on Our Fathers Will (Love) and being Grateful is the key. By saying "thank you" for everything we accept that we are always being blessed with exactly what we need and protected from what we don't need.

Like electrical currents, separately our feelings don't do much but when united our positive and negative feelings produce our chakra's energy systems. The opposites of Attracting and Repelling cancel one another until they are united with the opposites of Caring and Grateful. Together these feeling qualities produce powerful creative energy systems. Heart Dances return us to our true selves, to our most natural, original states of being purely present.

The 4th Heaven's Angel of Adulthood expresses the Dance of Caring, (*"I am Repelling, Attracting, Caring & Grateful"*). As healthy adults we seek to honor our deepest caring by attracting the right education, job, tools, habits, skills, friends, and partner while repelling the wrong ones. We empower our authentic,

Child of God selves by letting go of anything or anyone that does not honor our true caring. Our reward for succeeding is living a life for which we are grateful.

Sadly, in our world heathy, supportive, and nurturing childhoods are rare. So, as adults many of us heal our lacking childhood self-confidence with therapies and other dangerous initiations. As children everything new requires us to discern who and what we can trust. Adults with insecure inner children have poor judgement (discernment) and trust irresponsibly resulting in poor choices. Worse than that, childhood low self-esteem compels us to rely on the promises of lying predators and energy vampires.

Children who are fortunate enough to be appropriately valued and respected as children are free to follow their heart's feeling guidance. Healthy children become healthy adults who evolve through the same challenges that defeat those with low self-esteem. Few of us have the strength to acknowledge ourselves as the creators of our own unique realities. Heart Dances guide us to develop this strength faster, more efficiently and with less emotional pain than anything I know of.

The Fifth Heaven

The 5th Heaven's Angels of Communing and Elderhood guide us to open our Throat Chakra. This heaven's yoga is Mantra Yoga, the yoga of sound as its prayer, ("*Holy is your name*") describes. In Mantra Yoga God's "Name" is the original biblical "Word" who "was with God and was God" and said, "Let there be light" launching this creation. In Mantra Yoga this "Word" is often described as the "*Sound Current*," which breathing Mantras like Heart Dances attune to. With Mantra Yoga we learn to ride this current back to its Source. Attuning to our Creator's will in this way we feel touched by God's Joy for the return of His lost child.

The 5th heaven's Heart Dance, the *Dance of Communing* is, *"I am Listening (breathing in), Speaking (out), Communing (in), & Joyful (out)"*. In this dance as in Mantra Yoga we surrender to God's loving presence in ways that enable us to experience our lives as our creations. In this dance we let go to commune with our loving Source's creative essence who empowers our thoughts and words.

LISTENING: Listening is our first step towards communing. We Listen to connect with the Creator in us which naturally makes us more efficient creators. Here we discover how our unique illusions of time and space compel us to discern the truths within our own lies and the lies within our truths.

I've been blessed to experience quite a few births and the exquisite openness of our infant children and grandchildren. The ways they drink in their fresh new lives is mesmerizing. In their extreme states of letting go they are spectacularly present as if their every cell is listening to everything all at once. And that's a rather good description of Mantra Yoga. This is the magical holographic, omnipresent awareness, which we are all born with is what the Dance of Communing helps us to remember and develop.

Our lives present many choices. Some positive, some negative and *"one person's medicine is another's poison."* Some envision a one size fits all world where they gain total control by erasing our individuality. If such a world were possible it would be Hell but fortunately it's not possible. The Hell they imagine cannot exist because it's beyond unnatural requiring countless lies, wars, and endless suffering. Stripping away our unique identities to satisfy their inflated egos. Their efforts to create a new more convenient human as if God were a screwup is insane.

We have allowed their insanity to program our children and our subconscious minds is impressive. TVs, advertising, fictitious histories, and planned disasters have been effective controls. But learning from our choices and creations is what we're designed for, and they've taught us a lot. Their nefarious plans compel us to listen, and our survival depends on it. Fortunately, their plans go against God's plan for us and that's what some of us are beginning to hear. Both plans require us to surrender but in one we are expected to surrender to our fears and in the other we are being invited to surrender to love. Sadly, many of us are being held captive in their matrix of lies. But "saying no" to them isn't the whole answer, saying yes to our own natural states of freedom is how the freedom we all seek is realized.

We do this by listening holographically, and we do that with our hearts, as young Solomon did. Heart-felt listening is how Solomon attracted his legendary wealth and power. But later in life Solomon was seduced by the same dark controlling arts that began the decline of Judaism. Dark magic is the reason so many of us are suffering now and listening to our hearts is how we fix it. That's our big lesson right now!

Lacking the healthy self-esteem needed for listening to and following our hearts instead of our puppet leaders, or so-called authorities, and their false god, 'money.' The strength and ability to follow our hearts are the gifts we give to ourselves by embracing them as we do in Heart Dances. Having more wealth than any previous generation and yet being less happy is how our current generation is telling us to listen. Our current condition, being so close to self-extinction, is entirely about not listening and not making our own authentic choices. It's our egos pretending to believe we know that prevents us from listening to our hearts divine knowing. Our hearts close saying, *"No this is not for you"* or open saying, *"Yes this is for you"* and yesterday's "yes" is often today's no.

SPEAKING: Speaking includes all our forms of expression. Talking, singing, and dancing, drawing, sculpting, thinking, and imagining are all ways of Speaking. We listen to receive information and speak to share the same. The most valuable, the rarest and most useful information we have is about how we create. And our most valuable insights reveal what we genuinely want to create.

Knowing our purpose enables us to create it consciously. We create our purpose by returning to the beginning of everything, to the "Word." By expressing ourselves as God did. We "Let there be light," honoring our Highest Truth. We are the "Light of the World" so that is our purpose, to express The Light that we are. Before teaching his prayer Jesus warned against *"Vain Repetitions,"* which is speaking without feeling or purpose. As conscious conduits of Our Father's Love we dance to express, "Let there be light." By Speaking, thinking, and feeling these Heart Dances we replace our survivor's negative creations with our inner creator's positive ones. Speaking is how we move our thoughts into a feeling reality.

COMMUNING: We listen and speak, communicating to realize our true common union with one another to create healthy communities. In our Throat Chakra we transcend our survivor's negative awareness. Here we Commune by *Listening* to discover and *'Speaking'* to reveal. Our goal here is to realize our agreements and honor our soul's deepest memory of our origin in the 'Heart of God.'

The Church I grew up in celebrated *Holy Communion*. By consuming the "Body of Christ" symbolized by consecrated wafers of bread they said we could commune with Christ. This promised sacred experience of Divine Union with Christ is a notable example of how the best lies are mostly true. The experience they promise is the one we all want, only it has nothing to do with bread consecrated by the ordained priests of the purported "only true church."

Communion with Christ within us is the promise and purpose of all spiritual exercises. The spiritual technology of Christ Consciousness is still embedded in the foundations of religions who have forgotten their sacred purpose and ours. Having forgotten how to commune with Christ in us is the primary cause of suffering and the confused haunting emptiness that compels us to look for 'Love' in all the wrong places.

It's the technology of letting go to go to commune with our own purest, true inner selves that organized religions attempt to control. Ironically, there's always more to let go of because that's what we are here to learn. To know ourselves as an endless spectrum of the Light of Christ leading to our Souls Center, is endless. With each letting go we progress into a deeper Holy Communion with our own Sacred Essence. In Holy Communion we experience ourselves as Love's vessels and co-creative instruments.

JOYFUL: The result of Holy Communion with God in us is feeling Joyful. Joy is the experience of touching and being touched by *Pure Love*. Joy rises from our Heart to our Throat Chakras like bubbles of champaign to be felt, expressed, shared, and savored. Like its cousin happiness, Joy is infectious. Joy is our Throat Chakra's pure letting go, surrendering our ego's agendas to know our Creator's Will, bringing our most sacred thoughts and feelings to life. Joy expresses our enjoyment of touching, being touched and feeling loved. Our needs are the openings through which

Love touches us. Love fulfills our needs, effortlessly touching, healing, fulfilling, and awakening us. Our Soul's celebration of fulfillment, of being healed, awakened, and saved by the Savior in us is Joy.

Our Throat Chakra's Heart Dance, the "Dance of Communing" is ("I am Listening, I am Speaking, I am Communing & I am Joyful) expresses Mantra Yoga. In this dance we listen and speak to commune with God producing powerfully liberating experiences of using the Law of Attraction consciously and efficiently. By arranging special words into special patterns, in Heart Dances we channel the Original Word that awakens and empowers the creator in us. In Heart Dances as in Mantra Yoga we bask in our loving Creator's presence. The prayer here is, ("*Holy is your name*") also describing Mantra Yoga wherein special words often called "*Names of God*" are used to attune to God's presence, called "The Sound Current" within us.

Elderhood is our time for sharing the gifts we've discovered and developed during Adulthood. The Elder's mantra, "*Healer Heal Thy Self*" is about encouraging others to heal themselves by sharing our own experiences of healing. Our wounded inner-children's unheard cries are the seeds of suffering, which Elders embrace as healing opportunities for letting go. True Elders guide us to create openings that

Love naturally fills. Elders listen, speak, and commune to honor and empower the inner creator-child who most of us experience as our weakness, but in fact is the part of us most connected to our 'Source' or God.

"Joy comes from touching and from being touched by the goodness or God-ness of anyone or anything."
"The nature of heaven is like that of a child." We do not need to understand or speak His language to dance with him."

From Bodie McCoy's book 'Heart Dances" page 78

Our 6th Heaven's gate is within our 3rd Eye. It's Angels of Seeing and of Elderhood guide us to open this gate with Yantra Yoga. Yantra Yoga reveals the inner *Truth of Unity* within the outer *Illusion of Separation*, which Jesus described saying, "*Let your eye be single and your whole body will be filled with light.*" Yantra guides us to look through our Christ/Soul's eyes.

The 6th Heaven's prayer, "*In Heaven*", focuses through our 3rd Eye as Yantra Yoga does. By looking into the heavenly reality within this gate we dissolve our illusions into peaceful unity.

The 6th heaven's Heart Dance is the *Dance of Seeing* ("*I am Negating (breathing in), Affirming (out), Seeing (in), & Peaceful (out)*", guides us to be in God's loving presence, here and now.

NEGATING: Negating is saying "No," creating space for something more or better. It's also seeing the negative side of things. Survivors Negate defensively amplifying the illusion, which naturally makes us feel even more vulnerable. Creators Negate creatively making a place for Love to fulfill. Our survivor makes our lives emptier, lonelier, and more dangerous. Our inner creator makes our lives freer, more abundant, more connected, and more loving.

Saying no to things, people, and conditions that we do not want, or need is a beautiful form of self-love. Negating what detracts from our happiness or wellbeing is being true to ourselves and that is our first obligation here. *"To thy own self be true"* is the empowering wisdom that encourages us to listen and follow our hearts. By saying no to unloving choices, to weaknesses, lies, and dangers we honor ourselves. Often those who want us to say yes most, are the ones most blessed most when we say. By strengthening our abilities to negate we become spiritual warriors.

For humanity's sake it's crucial to exercise the wisdom to say "No" to those who would control us. As their cunning lies, deceptions and threats are being exposed we must respond by honoring our soul's sacred oaths to be present, free and authentic. Dark illusions of control dissolving in the radiance of this New Galactic Day are providing us with unprecedented opportunities for letting go and freedom. This is our time to liberate ourselves by saying "No."

We've been programed to allow the criminally insane amongst us to have their way. Through our inability to say no on our own behalf, we've accepted their massive lies, thefts, and murders. Failing to say "no" we've allowed them to weaponize every aspect of our world. Our religions, our health care system, our schools, entertainment, our food, air, water, and weather are all being used to distract, control, weaken and neutralize us. Their expressed end game is even to reduce Earth's population to 500,000,000. Not only have we not said "no," but most of us haven't even acknowledged their nefarious plans to enslave us by feeding into our doubts, fears, and base desires from cradle to grave. Their arrogant plans go against nature, who they also intend to enslave. But to succeed they need our permission, which we have given freely. They need us to say 'Yes' but with the veils lifting it is now the time we need to say 'No' to them and 'Yes' to what is for the Highest Good of all!

AFFIRMING: Affirming is saying "Yes," positively expressing approval. Where "No" restricts our survivor, "Yes" liberates our creator. By negating what we don't want and affirming what we do want we focus our creative awareness. "Yes" is superior to No as it affirms our creator who is superior to our negating survivor. "Yes," is the courier of the oaths that flow through the creative pathways, which we open by saying "No." In Heart Dances we affirm Love and Negate our survivors fears.

Affirming is looking for the blessing and creative opportunity within everything and everyone. We are empowered as creators by saying yes to the goodness in anyone or anything that seems to have caused us suffering. Affirming God's will as our own, saying yes to the Light within us, makes our oaths and agreements effective tools for reclaiming and rebuilding our essential Humanness. Much as light devours darkness saying "Yes" to our own goodness dispels our fears.

SEEKING/SEEING: What we seek we affirm and looking for what we want or avoiding what we don't want distorts our creative awareness. Looking towards what we want we affirm it, and looking away we negate it. This is our survivor's controlling nature, which we transcend by affirming, and negating equally without prejudice. By looking within, we penetrate the holographic illusion to see our innermost truth of Unity, AKA Love.

Through two eyes we see the outer holographic illusion of duality. Through our 3rd Eye we see to experience what Jesus described when he said, "*Let your eye be single and your whole body will be filled with light*". Light is liberated by the Unity of Opposites, which we accomplish by letting go to "*let* our eye be single" as we do in the *Dance of Seeing*.

PEACEFUL: When we seek peace, the more we do, the less peaceful we are. In our stories enemies are defeated, we fall in love, get rich, dreams come true, and we live happily ever after. Those stories are about survivor's stories who never truly win or find lasting peace. A survivor's search for peace through control, which is exhausting and ends in failure, also presents lots of opportunities for letting go. Unfortunately, those opportunities are generally sacrificed to play the Name Game.

We find Peace when we stop seeking and simply see that there is nothing missing, nothing to improve and nothing to seek. Seeing reveals The Creator's perfection everywhere, in everyone, especially in us and in our unique lives. Seeing God's perfection brings us to Peace and the permission to be present as ourselves. Focusing through our 3rd Eye opens our Mental Body to be filled with light illuminating how God's will, to "Let there be light" defines Reality, including us as magical beings, shrouded in ordinariness.

The 6th Heaven's Heart Dance, the "Dance of Seeing" ("I am *Negating*, I am *Affirming*, I am *Seeing* & I am *Peaceful*), expresses Yantra Yoga, which resonates with our 3rd Eye. Our inner creator Negates and Affirms to See God's ever-present perfection or

Heaven, AKA *Peace*. Survivors playing it safe by expecting God to prove his love are naturally disappointed. A survivor often experiences God's love as disillusioning as their beliefs and desires are lovingly stripped away. A creator trusting in God's perfection welcomes disillusionment as liberation, even when it hurts. Or if they feel betrayed, creators willingly let their illusions go. The differences between a survivor suffering and a creators ecstasy are defined by their relationships with the illusions they seek.

To be present we let our past and future illusions go. This is the foundational teaching of all true religions and spiritual traditions. The prayer of this heaven, "*In Heaven*" means "In the present," which is the first thing Jesus taught. He said, "*Repent for the Kingdom of God (Heaven) is at hand.*" Survivors hear a threat warning them of Hell or Evil, which is the holographic illusion that separates us from the present and ourselves. In the same words creators hear the beautiful, hopeful promise that the peaceful heaven we all seek is here right now.

We come to the present by letting go of our seeking to simply see, which is what Yantra Yoga and the Dance of Seeing guide us to do. The Dance of Seeing reveals the Angel of Elderhood's presence in this heaven. Elderhood is our time to share the gifts and abilities that we've discovered and honed as adults. By positively Negating (saying No) and Affirming (saying Yes) we See God's perfection within ourselves and in creations magical mirror. As loving elders, we accelerate Humanities evolution by sharing our ways of loving and healing our inner child's "I am not" illusions. As elders our eyes and theirs are opened as we peacefully see "They are" as opportunities to love them as we love ourselves.

"To enter the inner kingdom of God's consciousness, while still living in this world is like walking on water. The practical world does not want to lose such a valuable citizen so it will try hard to discourage you. To succeed you will need to affirm yourself as Gods child and negate the seductions, pleadings and demands of your outer environment. Only a mature elder can do this responsibly and without ego."

Quote by Bodie McCoy from 'The Eight Heaven" page 38.

The 7th Heaven's gate within our Crown Chakra is opened by its Angels of *Accomplishing* and *Mastery*. The 7th Heaven's yoga Raja, the "Royal Yoga" guides us to embody our royal heritage. Upon our Crown Chakra we wear "hats" that identify our *Accomplishments.* Raja guides us to dawn our of our inner Christs Crown also called our *halo* and our soul's light, which we let shine by allowing our Merkabah Light Bodies to spin freely.

The 7th Heaven's prayer, *"Our Father"*, identifies our royalty as the King of King's children. Here the *Dance of Accomplishing* affirms, *"I am Controlling (breathing in), I am Liberating (out), I am Accomplishing (in), & I am Free (out)."* In this dance we identify as God's highest accomplishment; *"Created in his own image and likeness"* we are also creators, naturally responsible for our unique realities.

CONTROLLING: As our favorite illusion 'Control' exists nowhere in nature it is unsustainable. Our survivors' unnatural dreams of control are the cornerstone of our 'Might Makes Right' world. Striving to accomplish our collective dreams of peace with hellish wars has led us to create weapons capable of ending life on Earth as we know it. The fact that we haven't realized war doesn't work is a testimony to how powerful our survivors' fears affect us.

The saber rattling persists as globalists continue envisioning total control over everything and everyone. As Milton expressed in *Paradice Lost*; our egos struggle to play God, which is impossible, rather than cocreating with God as we are designed to. One approach is true, and the other is false. One works and one doesn't. One approach makes our lives blessed and easy and the other makes our lives more difficult as we struggle to swim against the flow of our Father's will.

Our fool's choice to trade something so real and good for something so false has produced our destructive world. To our inner creator, controlling is focusing our creative awareness to attract what we want and repel what we don't. Though our survivors believe in controlling our outer lives, our creator works to create the experiences that our outer lives reflect. By the time we attract something we've already experienced its promise. Focusing on what we want feels good and focusing on what we don't want doesn't feel good. As God's Children we follow our heart's feelgood guidance.

Love naturally attracts what we need, and fear naturally attracts what we fear. Creators focus on what they want, and survivors react, perpetuating what they don't want. One approach leads to freedom and the other is slavery.

Survivors' efforts to control their outer lives compel them to energize their outer illusions of separation, fueling their fears of isolation, abandonment, unworthiness, and ineffectiveness. Our survivors' fears undermine our efforts to unite in love, while our responsible creator's focus dissolves our fears and the illusions they promote. As we allow our creator's love to guide our choices our dreams are fulfilled magically, effortlessly. A survivor's struggles for control are both futile and extremely wasteful. We may easily see how their defensive wars and machines are devouring our Mother Earth. Worse, our survivor's efforts are our future and our only way out of this destructive nightmare is to know ourselves as the creators of our own unique realities; by thinking, believing, feeling, and living as creators.

Currently our survivor's ways are so deeply imprinted in our hearts, our minds, and institutions to change all that seems impossible. For the defensive power of numbers, survivors we've gathered in likeminded groups, clubs, religions, and organizations. Our survivor's efforts to establish superiority by controlling one another permeates every facet of our lives. But it all begins with our thinking, so this is what we must change.

Historically our efforts to control have failed so completely that now it is obvious; our survival depends on our willingness to think and create in completely new ways. That's going to take a while, but the benefits of focusing in this new way are available to us from the moment we sincerely commit ourselves to this new human experiment. For example, stop focusing on future goals as we always have as the primary goal is to be present. Now is our time to "*Repent* (change our approach) *for the Kingdom of God* (Heaven) *is at hand* (in the present).

LIBERATING: The opposite of Controlling is Liberating. Controlling is holding on and Liberating is Letting go. Controlling is restrictive, Liberating is freeing. The opposite of focusing is defocusing, which is what we do in meditation, in prayer and in both Mantra and Yantra Yogas. When we defocus our awareness naturally moves from creation to its Creator, who is Love.

To liberate ourselves from the prevailing insanity we must learn to focus differently. It is both simple and yet challenging to think differently than the majority. Ironically, it may even feel like we are betraying our own souls purpose to know unity on earth as we do within our inner heavens, but it is the opposite. We betrayed our sacred purpose long ago, so the shift we must make now is our time to liberate ourselves from many lifetimes of our inner survivors' dividing thoughts, deeds, creations, and negative karma. What our survivors experience as failure and weakness our creator consciousness experiences as accomplishments and precious freedom.

As we accept creative responsibility for our lives our survivor's irrational guilt dissolves and a brilliant sanity is born. Our ability to liberate and heal our broken hearts begins as we choose to accept creative responsibility for everything in our lives. Literally every word, action, and re-action!

The work ahead of us presents great opportunities for personal growth and cultural evolution through being of service to one another. To help others liberate themselves from our survivor's confining web we begin by liberating ourselves, by letting go. Even as our peers pressure us to think as they do, we must think, act, and create in this new way.

To liberate ourselves now we must see how we are confined and enslaved by our own mind and beliefs. Our world is owned and controlled by rich and powerful sociopaths and narcissists who reflect our own thinking and desires. Blaming them for our problems may feel safer than accepting responsibility for them ourselves but blame is our survivor's game. By blaming them we empower them as we always have. By blaming ourselves, by accepting creative responsibility for our lives we affirm and empower ourselves as the creators of our realities.

ACCOMPLISHING: In our current world it is by our accomplishments that we liberate ourselves. With our worldly accomplishments we earn money and credentials, which are the passports our world requires before we are allowed to move freely through it. That's the promise but it's a lie. Those passports are created by and used to control us by those who have created them. More than this, the freedom, safety, and abundance they promise is also a lie. In that world we are never totally free.

Our leaders and the billionaires who control them are not the problem. They are in fact the least free of us all. That's not to say we should pity them, but we should learn from their sad stories about what works and what doesn't. To do this, to learn from our history, we must realize that for the most part the winners have written history. And who are they? They have been and still are the most greedy, ruthless, dishonest, arrogant, and controlling and hard hearted amongst us.

To know the liberating truth about ourselves and our history we must begin by accepting how we have created our unique realities. We must accept that for all this time we have been creators living as survivors. The heroes of our stories are survivors because survivors have written them. They have been written in our hearts, our minds, and historical records for much longer than any of us can remember. Survivors, survivalist stories have been poured into our open childhood hearts and minds. And we see them everywhere we look because we are creators still living as survivors, and still creating our survivor's stories. To make our shifts from survivors to creators we must begin seeing ourselves in this new way and begin telling new stories, creator stories. By telling our stories as their creators we exercise the new creator's freedom that experientially accelerates the forgiveness that we need to begin our healing. Healing and forgiveness will soon become the heart of our thoughts, work, and activities. Healing, forgiveness, loving and caring will become the measure of our Accomplishments.

FREE: Thinking as outwardly focused survivors we see freedom primarily in physical ways. Accumulating material wealth has been a goal of many revered citizens. Accumulating material wealth, physical freedom and strengths are the stuff many of our dreams are made of. The creators' dreams are made of the freedom to simply be present, to be here and now, "in Heaven."

A survivor's physical dreams are made of burdensome possessions and powers to control others. especially their enemies. A creator who possesses the ability to create what he or she wants must only consider the question of "What do you want?" The more considerate we are the more we realize how our relationships reflect our relationships with ourselves. The ultimate Freedom, the Freedom to always be in love, to be free to love everyone and everything is the freedom to always be present. This is the creator's dream that we realize by loving ourselves.

As we let go to Freely embody our Child of God Soul-Self, we accept our own royal authority over our unique realities. We affirm our royal freedom in the *"Dance of Accomplishing,"* ("I am *Controlling*, I am *Liberating*, I am *Accomplishing* & I am *Free)*. This is Raja or Royal Yoga, which resonates with our Crown Chakra. By affirming Controlling (focusing) and Liberating (letting go) we dance to exercise our innate Freedom to be our loving selves. Freedom, however, isn't our goal. It is this way of thinking that leads us to it. With Heart Dances, we give ourselves permission to be present, to pursue happiness, while respecting the rights of others to do the same.

Our Crown Chakra's prayer ("*Our Father*") raises the question of, "*What does it mean to be God's Children?*" What does it mean to be created in the "likeness" of the all-powerful, Unconditionally Loving, ever-present Creator of everything? Jesus answered this essential question in the first two words of his prayer. By describing God and us with the same two words he expressed our Soul's reality, "*I and my Father are One.*" When Jesus said, "I am my Father's *only* Son" he expressed the reality of the Christ AKA our Soul's-Awareness.

The Angel of Mastery's presence in the Seventh Heaven may be observed in its "Dance of Accomplishing" ("I am *Controlling*, I am *Liberating*, I am *Accomplishing* & I am *Free*"). Mastery is about living as Jesus and others have in earthly bodies while also in heavenly Soul-Awareness. Here we learn to assume our roles of spiritual leadership by accepting creative responsibility for our own creative inner awareness. Then we may experience our outer lives as our inner lives' reflections.

The only true mastery is Self-Mastery, which develops our focus (control) to liberate us to discover ourselves as our own greatest accomplishments. Then it's simple, the best use of our lives is growing more self-aware. Then we naturally begin to learn how we are created and how we create, and naturally we become better creators. The freedom to create as we want and what we want is the Freedom of Mastery.

"The seventh Heart Dance moves us beyond our individual identity. Here all our needs to accomplish or succeed are revealed as one big lie. Accomplishing to receive positive attention just validates that big lie. The world will always know you by your accomplishments and praise feels good but it's just a reflection. Dance with that reflection long enough and you will think it's you but touch your image in a mirror. Do you receive any satisfaction? I doubt it. Only dancing with God liberates us to be just as He created us and in the seventh dance we move beyond the limits of our thoughts and senses to the truth of who we are. This is free."

Quote by Bodie McCoy from his book 'Heart Dances" page 81.

The 8th Heaven's gate is within our Spiritual Heart Chakra whose Angels of *Accomplishing* and *Mastery* teach us through this narrow gate. This is the New Heaven that many more of us are awakening to now. This is where we realize what being created in the "Image and likeness of our Creator" truly means. Jesus was obviously a pioneer in guiding us to occupy this center but there have certainly been others.

The 8th heaven's yoga, Bhakti Yoga, guides us to devote ourselves to God's Unconditionally Loving presence within us. Our Spiritual Heart Chakra is where our purest love resides and is what Jesus expressed saying, "*I and my Father are One*." We see this *Sacred Heart* that we see in many portraits of Jesus. Bhakti Yoga guides us to let go to know our inner Christ, our purely loving True Self.

The 8th Heaven's prayer is again, "*Our Father*". In our crown chakra attunement "Our Father" affirms us as the King of King's children. Here as our Spiritual Heart attunement, it affirms God's presence within us. Our Spiritual Heart's *Dance of Awareness*, [*"I am Consuming (breathing in), Creating (out), Aware (in), & Loving (out)"*] expresses the Godly qualities that empower us to create our unique realities as "god's" (small g).

CONSUMING: This dance's first step affirms our Soul's *"Consuming"* nature. God appeared to Moses as the Burning Bush and to Jesus' disciples as "Tongues of Fire." Like our heavenly Father, our human Soul is an All-Consuming Flame. The Mayas call the black hole at the heart of our galaxy, *"Hunab Ku," "God of the Central Sun"* who both consumes and creates our galaxies stars. How we deal with our own consuming nature determines what we create.

A survivor's outwardly focused consuming nature can't get enough because the outer illusion isn't real. The promises we see out there are all false but to our survivor they are convincing. It's our own All Consuming Flame nature that frightens us. That's ok as to engage its endless brilliance and appetites before accepting creative responsibility for our lives leads us to countless addictions and destructive behaviors.

We consume vast amounts of air. We consume vast amounts of water, food, information, and energy. Of course, our consuming nature has been manipulated by those who would control us by controlling the things they've convinced us we need to enjoy good lives. Their false promises misdirecting our consuming nature currently have us devouring our beautiful planet and this will only stop as accept creative responsibility for our lives.

CREATING: Being creators' means being conscious of what we give our attention to and why. It is realizing that our hearts follow our minds, therefore happy thoughts create happy feelings. It is also recognizing the results of the thoughts we hold and asking if that's what we want to feel. It is seeing how our feelings grow, attract, and manifest as the conditions, abilities and relationships that seemingly define us. Being a creator is realizing how the thoughts and feelings that we choose define us and therefore the lives we create.

Of course, our goal is to create more of what we want and less of what we don't, it is that simple. As creators we get to choose to let things be simple or make them complicated. But it's impossible to let things be when we don't know what we want and all the while TV, school, religions, doctors, leaders, teachers, friends, families and even our own physical senses are telling us what we should and shouldn't want. Being a creator is embracing the living principles we all share and realizing how these principles invite us to see, believe and create as we choose.

Believing false promises and seeing only what we want to see are ways we create addictions and ways we choose to avoid our creative responsibilities. With these choices we sacrifice our freedoms. Regardless of our choices we are the creators of our own one-of-a-kind kind realities whose creator-souls guide our unique creative purposes. To see or hear our soul's loving guidance we must be still to see and listen into our own hearts, which is challenging when our "Information Age" is offering us ten answers to every imaginable question.

Being a creator is accepting how all our needs flow through channels of awareness. A conscious creator grows aware of how our awareness flows to the Creator and is returned for our highest good.

AWARENESS: Quantum Physics is finally realizing that the whole universe is an interconnected web of awareness. Even what we have seen as empty space is alive and full of awareness. This reminds me of Spider's presence is the Daath design, which I see as an expression of the importance of our creative webs of awareness. As we enter this level of our consciousness, we begin to see how our webs of awareness are produced by our thoughts and feelings. The more aware we become of how we create the more we begin to appreciate the values of our creative webs.

Some eastern religions teach valuable insights into how our creative awareness reflects God's creative awareness. To understand how awareness creates us and creates through us it's important to acknowledge its two sides. In the East they call them Yin and Yang. We tend to think of them more as positive and negative energies also called Male and Female. The strong feelings and beliefs we have about these seemingly opposed energies prevent us from seeing their beautiful dance.

One useful Eastern understanding of these opposites says that everything is made of them including us. Men they say wear their Yang maleness on the outside so on the inside they are Yin or feminine. Women who wear their Yin femaleness on the outside are Yang or Male on the inside. So, women are physically more vulnerable and sensitive but inwardly they are strong. And men who are physically stronger are inwardly, emotionally more sensitive, and vulnerable.

This human design explains why women are emotionally stronger and why men often harden their hearts. The reason our design seemingly works against us, making our relationships difficult, is our prejudice. Our Might Makes Right world still values men more than women because they are physically stronger, and our values are largely physical. Today we know that everything is made of aware energies. As that sinks in our values will shift from primarily physical to spiritual (energy) and this is something that doing Heart Dances guides us to develop.

Heart Dances allow us to feel how these opposites dance within us melting our survivor's prejudices. As we dance, we grow more aware of how balance governs us and everything. With this understanding we learn to ride these energies, to embody the empowering sparks of their unions. As we let our awareness flow more freely.

LOVING: Love is the Great Mystery who is impossible to control or to find but is everywhere, in everyone, everything it every breath. Love is not something we can ever understand or do but Love is who we are. We both want and fear Love who is the attractor that creates, balances, and rules the whole universe. Love is the creative light who empowers us by manifesting our thoughts and feelings. Love who unites all opposites is the healer, the only. who cannot be possessed but can only be attracted by letting go. So, the only way to Love is by letting go.

I met the love of my life, Barbara, one minute after prayerfully informing God that I was done with women. The moment I looked into Barbara's eyes I forgot that prayer and I didn't remember it again till years later. I was reflecting on the greatest blessings of my life. I was hoping to understand how I'd created all those blessings, especially Barbara. I asked to see what they all might have in common, and it was so obvious. All those blessings were experiences of being loved and all were preceded by experiences of letting go. That's why they call it "Falling I love."

A survivor's material values cause him or her to confuse love with material gifts, which prevents them truly knowing either. Survivors' pursuits never lead to the present and looking for love in the wrong places makes their lives painful. Feeling deeply disappointed and unrewarded makes us feel like there is something wrong with us when in truth we are merely misguided. Again, the ultimate freedom is to always be in love. The freedom to love everyone and everything evades and leaves us wanting, until we let go. Love, having no price, is impossible to earn or deserve. It is life's precious gift. However, love does require us to let go, to be fully present where love resides. This is our greatest challenge as our mind and its external focus on all life's distraction take us out of the present. Working with Heart Dances is a dynamic technique for coming into the present. Being present in our loving is our deepest spiritual strength.

Our Spiritual Heart's, *"Dance of Awareness is,"* ("I am *Consuming*, I am *Creating*, I am *Aware* & I am *Loving)* expresses an experience of Bhakti Yoga quite different than our Emotional Heart's dance. Our Emotional Hearts open gratefully, and our Spiritual Hearts opens in Love. Gratitude is feeling loved and being in love is our highest, truest most loving selves. On this level we practice Bhakti Yoga, the Yoga of devotion, by devoting ourselves to the Source of our true loving nature, God who is Love.

By consciously Consuming and Creating we grow Aware of Loving as both who we are and what we want. This agreement empowers us to create from our hearts and grow more Aware of how Love creates and consumes as it dances through us and our lives. As we experience Love as the capstone of Human Consciousness, we grow to see Love is our highest goal and letting go is how we achieve it. Jesus used the attunement (*"Our Father"*) for both our Crown and Spiritual Heart Chakras identifying the sameness of our inner creator and the Creator and the holographic reality wherein, "Loving God, our neighbor and ourselves" are the same.

Jesus said, *"I am my Father's only Son"* expressing Christ's Soul-Awareness.

The Angel of Mastery's presence in the Eighth Heaven is expressed in its "Dance of Awareness" ("I am *Consuming*, I am *Creating*, I am *Aware* & I am *Loving*"). The leadership of Mastery here is about being the example by embodying the qualities of our Creator. Self-Mastery on this level develops our abilities to *consume*, *create*, to be *aware* and *loving*. Here we are truly liberated.

In the Sun Cross Codex *God's Light* is illustrated by *Hunab* Ku, centered in the image below. It is an amazing two-dimensional representation of how God created us. From the center outward it shows our His light dividing to produce our subconscious and conscious minds. These divide into our 4 light-bodies and again to produce our 8 chakras and the 16 conscious and 16 subconscious polarities. These produce our Merkabah-light-body's 32 faces, which divide into our 64 DNA chromosomes, 128 perceptions and 256 patterns of attachment and resistance. The codex shows us how our holographic awareness is produced by dividing and reuniting the opposites in us. This is how our own true nature guides us to produce peaceful unity by letting go through the *Unity of Opposites*.

The cleansing breaths, heartfelt affirmations, and awakening rebirthing experiences Heart Dances provide, replace the minds' disappointing and limited sense of reality. By letting go we surrender to the holographic reality of the universe, wherein each pixel contains the whole. So, I am in you, you are in me, and God is in us all. This is what spiritual teachers have been saying forever and I remember when this sounded crazy to me. Our physical senses, and our minds ego, all experience the outer illusions that most of us call 'reality.' But there's so much more! With Heart Dances we dance between the illusions of our mind and our soul's unconditionally loving awareness. The mind struggles to see life the way it wants it to be. Our soul sees it as it is. 'Heart Dances' retrain the mind to process life as it is rather than how we 'think it should be.' This is the pathway to unconditional love and true freedom.

When asked, "*What is the greatest commandment*" Jesus said, "*To love God with all your heart* (feelings), *all your mind* (thoughts) *and all your soul* (awareness) *this is the first and great commandment. And the second one is like it, to love your neighbor as yourself.*" Here Jesus implies the holographic reality wherein we love God by loving our neighbor as ourselves, because deep down he, or she, is our 'Self.' Holographically, we love God and our neighbor by loving ourselves. With the gift of attention, we claim the holographic freedom to live our lives loving everything. Embracing Gods' creation as perfect.

By letting go we come to the present where our illusions of past and future do not exist. In the Codex we see Pakal and Chan Bahlam illustrating Christ's first teaching after his baptism by John. He said *"Repent (let go) for the Kingdom of God is at hand* (in the present)."* By interpreting this beautiful promise as a threat many have missed both Jesus' useful advice and beautiful promise. He promises us that Heaven is right here, right now, not just for the "good (obedient)" ones. When we react to unresolved events from our past, we instantly project them into the future and miss the Heavenly present, where we all go when we let go.

Heart Dances™ lift us into the holographic present by spinning our Merkabah-light-bodies faster. Spin produces balancing vortexes that righten us spiritually like spinning tops or gyroscopes. Heaven is indeed up, not in the sky but above and beyond our polarized illusions of good and bad, right and wrong, here and there, or past and future. By

describing us and God in the first two words of his prayer Jesus reveals the holographic reality where, *"I and my Father are One."* This is Christ's Truth within all of us. We are the *"Light of the World,"* our Creator's holographic family of holographic creators, forged by His Will to *"Let there be Light."* Like the heart of Jesus' Prayer, Heart Dances guide us to experience *"God's Kingdom coming,"* as *"His Will is done, as in Heaven so also in Earth (in us)."*

Now take a moment to feel the Light within you with *"The Dance of Ascension."* Let go, come fully present in your inner heaven. *Receive* each breath fully and *let*

it go. Feel each word flowing to the next. Breathe and feel this inner dance in all your chakras (Base, Navel, Solar plexus, Heart, Throat, 3rd Eye, Crown & Spiritual Heart).

The 'Dance of Ascension' Word Chart:

*LETTING GO (out breath):	*BASE/SEXUAL CHAKRA
*ACCEPTING (in breath):	*NAVEL CHAKRA
*APPRECIATING (out breath)	*SOLAR PLEXUS CHAKRA
*GRATEFUL (in)	*HEART CHAKRA
*JOYFUL (out)	*THROAT CHAKRA
*PEACEFUL (in)	*3rd EYE CHAKRA
*FREE (out)	*CROWN CHAKRA
*LOVING (in breath & out breath)	*SPIRITUAL HEART

CHAPTER #22: SYNCHRONICITY AND A COIN CHART

Carl Jung coined a word to describe how we experience the holographic present. What most call *"Luck, Coincidence or Being in the right place at the right time"* Jung called *"Synchronicity."* Barb and I have experienced and witnessed synchronicity working through *"Oracle of the Heart™"* and its *Heart Dances™* time and time again. God's holographic, *"Law of Attraction"* says, *"As you think, in your heart (feelings) you shall be."* Happy thoughts produce happy feelings and unhappy thoughts produce unhappy ones. Letting go to *"Be in the right place at the right time"* is how we claim our god given natural freedom to create the reality we want. Our mind is a tool for us to do just that. But we tend to let it run us rather than us directing it. Give yourself permission to think how you want to feel, no matter where we are or what is happening around you. This is true freedom.

It takes courage to truly look within, to face ourselves, and to accept creative responsibility for our lives. Faith in the goodness of life itself, in God, Love, A Higher Power or whatever name you use to describe that which miraculously created all of this, is required.

One effective way of letting go, of surrendering to the magical holographic present, is described in Proverbs 16:33: It says, *"The die is cast into the lap, but every decision is from the Lord"*. By tossing a die or a coin we return our precious Free Will to our Creator utilizing his *Law of Attraction* optimally.

Try it for yourself and experience the perfection of what comes forth for you.

*Toss a coin 3 times to select an angel to guide your creative awareness today: (**H**= heads, **T**= tails):

- Angel #1= HHH   [heads, heads, heads]
- Angel #2= HHT   [heads, heads, tails]

- Angel #3= HTT   [heads, tails, tails]
- Angel #4= TTT   [tails, tails, tails]
- Angel #5= TTH   [tails, tails, heads]
- Angel #6= THH   [tails, heads, heads]
- Angel #7= HTH   [heads, tails, heads]
- Angel #8= THT   [tails, heads, tails]

Angel #1 BASE CHAKRA: (Page 44) *The Angel of Wanting*: RECEIVING (in), GIVING (out), WANTING (in), 4 LETTING GO (out):

Angel #2 NAVEL CHAKRA: (Page 47) *The Angel of Knowing*: DISCERNING (in), TRUSTING (out), KNOWING (in), ACCEPTING (out):

Angel #3 SOLAR PLEXUS CHAKRA: (Page 53) *The Angel of Responding*: UNHAPPY (in), HAPPY (in), RESPONDING (in), APPRECIATING (out) LEVEL:

Angel #4 HEART CHAKRA: (Page 56) *The Angel of Caring*: REPELLING (in), ATTRACTING (in), CARING (in), GRATEFUL (in):

Angel #5 THROAT CHAKRA: (Page 64) *The Angel of Communing*: LISTENING (in), SPEAKING (in), COMMUNING (in), JOYFUL (in):

Angel #6 THIRD EYE: (Page 67) *The Angel of Seeing*: NEGATING (in), AFFIRMING (in), SEEING (in), PEACEFUL (in):

Angel #7 CROWN CHAKRA: (Page 73) *The Angel of Accomplishing*: CONTROLLING (in), LIBERATING (in), ACCOMPLISHING (in), FREE(in):

Angle #8 SPIRITUAL HEART: (Page 77) *The Angel of Awareness*: CONSUMING (in), CREATING (out), AWARE (in), LOVING (out):

Using Synchronicity to select these angels will provide powerfully liberating personal insights for living each day wholeheartedly. Devotion is required to change the fundamental beliefs and choices deeply imprinted in our subconscious minds. This is especially challenging because our controlling egos and global 'Might Makes Right' culture is constantly telling us not to let go, not to trust ourselves or in the goodness [god-ness] of life.

Here, *"In the blink of God's eye"* we are all being changed. And thanks to the Mayan Tzolkin we understand how and why this is happening. The Mayan Ancient Ones identified this *"Eye"* as our Milky Way Galaxy, which viewed from the side appears to be blinking. *"The Blink"* is our Galaxy's *"Photon Belt,"* which is bathing us in Hunab Ku's most powerful energies.

Amongst the thousands of Pleiadean stars only 7 are *'Heavens'* and now, according to Mayan mythology, Earth is becoming the 8th Heaven, and we are changing fast. As our ego's illusions of control are dissolving those who resist get battered by the waves of change, and those who let go, get the ride of many lifetimes.

Most spiritual exercises today have traveled through ancient traditions and secret societies corrupted in the Underworlds over the last 26,000-year cycle. Heart Dances have emerged in this new era unfolding here and now, *"In the Blink"*, just as our spinning Merkabah's' are lifting us into the heavenly present like hot-air-balloons. We are ascending from our historic *"Seeing is believing"* reality to the *"Believing is seeing"* reality of the 8th Heaven.

When what we see defines what we believe, the material world we live in dictates our experiences. Historically trusting others more than we trust ourselves has not worked. We submit to their control by valuing the things they control more than ourselves. Creative freedom comes from valuing the blissful gems of our own consciousness. Knowing ourselves as creators liberates us to believe what we want to believe before we see it and create that!

Heart Dances™ teach us to value ourselves with the precious gift of our attention. If that sounds selfish it is not, it's being a responsible creator. In the 8th Heaven we realize 'Love' is the precious thing we all want most. Not the romanticized or commercialized illusions of love, but the 'Love' who flows through us eternally growing and attracting what we focus on.

In the Underworlds *"Our fears were visited upon us"* because fear was our focus. And what have we feared most? That life here on earth is some kind of prison sentence for something we don't even remember doing.

With Heart Dances™ we grow loving creative thoughts into feeling experiences of blissful, loving Soul

Awareness. As we let our attention flow naturally back to Love, magic happens. The Law of Attraction is an even exchange except when we give our loving awareness back to its Source, to God who is Love. This focus enhances everything in our lives indescribably and each person's experience is uniquely their own. Heart Dances enable you to evolve and ascend to higher and higher levels of awareness, uplifting every aspect of your life.

When Jesus said, *"Let your communication be Yes, Yes or No, No,"* he was speaking of how our hearts work as our creator's compass. An open heart says *"Yes,"* and a closed one says *"No"* and this is how our hearts lead us to Love. And keep in mind our hearts follow our minds. This is why it is so important to focus the mind on what is pure and sacred. As we align the mind with the pure qualities of light through the words that Heart Dances provide, we learn to trust the wisdom of our hearts and adapt to a new way of thinking! Our lives simplify, becoming peaceful, and yet highly productive.

Our hearts have been traumatized by our long dark journey through the Galactic Underworlds. Now our job is to heal them with love by focusing lovingly on all our feelings. In Heart Dances we *"Follow our hearts"* by focusing on our innate goodness. But in a world that identifies feelings as problems this is challenging. We all know this because 8 billion creators thinking and feeling like fearful survivors have created a multitude of problems. However, with 8 billion of us thinking loving thoughts, we can create *'Heaven on Earth.'* If you have been waiting for permission to be your best, most loving self this is it, the 8th Heaven is not happening to us. It is happening through us.

The 8th Heaven will be born as we *"Love our neighbors as ourselves"*. By helping them fulfill their needs we become Love's vessels and instruments. Our most urgent need now is to heal from lifetimes in the Underworlds. Earth's long timers are tired. We are done with our ego's greedy shortsighted shenanigans that have led us down this evolutionary cul-de-sac. It's time to accept *"We can't solve our problems with the same fearful thinking that created them."*

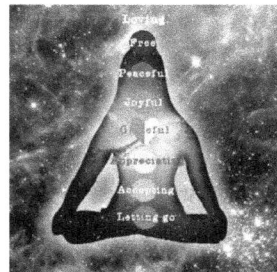

It's time to replace controlling thoughts with thoughts of:

Letting go (breathing out), **Accepting** (in), **Appreciating** (out), being **Grateful** (in), **Joyful** (out), **Peaceful** (in), **Free** (out) and **Loving** (in & out).

IN CONCLUSION

Angels of the Merkabah offer keys to the pearly gated heavens within us. They help replace our survivors limiting "*Seeing is Believing*" mindset with our inner creator's empowering "*Believing is Seeing*" one. Their Heart Dances™ guide us to occupy our Souls-Center and accept creative responsibility for our life by practicing the '*Art of Letting-go*' by uniting the opposites within us.

There is just one thing going on, and it's all about relationships. Our relationship with God, with our homes and communities, our friend's, families, with our enemies, even with food, and drink, are all reflections of our relationship with ourselves. *Heart Dances evolve our primary relationship with ourselves thus with everything and everyone*. Because we are creators, our life experiments respond to our intentions and beliefs. If we are looking for problems we will find them, and if we look for creative opportunities, we will find those!

We hope you experiment ongoingly with *Angels of the Merkabah* and their Heart Dances™ so you too will enjoy the immense benefits of learning to let go. They help us to evolve as we let go in order to reboot or restart our relationship with ourselves and to our lives. But the old seeing is believing program is deeply woven into the fabric of all our relationships so it takes practice!

Our entire world is programed in this outdated way, so we have a lot to do, and that too is good. The world and the Karma we've created is challenging us to evolve. You could even say that if we don't evolve, we threaten our own existence. If you are aware of how large and urgent our problems are you may also realize we absolutely require new ways of thinking to solve them. This is what 'Angels of the Merkabah' offer; utterly new ways of thinking that produce new ways of feeling, creating and being.

We heal our world with the holographic wisdom that says, *"Healer, heal thyself."*

 As you dedicate your use of Heart Dances to this purpose, you will begin to see miraculous improvements in your life; improvements in your health, in your finances, your relationships and in how you feel in general about everything. Many of these blessings are ones you will not even be aware of as they are the dodged bullets you never saw coming. What you will notice is the peaceful absence of drama and just plain feeling good.

The *"seeing is believing"* world sees *"success"* in terms of things like possessions, credentials, and money. And those who control those things use them to control us. The success this technology offers is to think, feel and attract what is for our Highest Good. The value of these heartfelt patterns of thought called Heart Dances lays in how they empower us to create by 'Believing to See.' What I've shared with you comes from my own experiences with Heart Dances that these Angels have revealed to me.

I find that working with Heart Dances first thing in the morning starts my day smoothly and happily. I like using a die, or our coin chart to select an angel to guide me through each day. I also do the *Dance of Ascension* every day. I find these fast and uncomplicated ways of balancing and centering myself lead to clearer perceptions, better choices, more enjoyment, and more satisfactory outcomes all around. Once you realize this, I believe you will also make these Angels and their Heart Dances your creative allies.

It has been our experience that sharing Heart Dances in groups is powerful. These days I like conference calls as these 'dances' happen entirely within oneself and sharing them can be uplifting not only for yourself but others. But any way of gathering to share Heart Dances connects and activates our Merkabah-light-bodies and here's the good part. When we dance together, we are all blessed by the energies and consciousness of our collective Merkabah.

At this moment it seems most useful with clearing and cleansing our self-defeating defensive programing. The job at hand is clearing our world's false *Might Makes Right* programing. And the clearer we get individually, the more we realize what we can do with it.

If you are looking at the mountains of challenges we are facing and thinking, *"What's the point? We're all screwed anyway!"* I promise that if you embrace the formidable *'Freedom is having nothing left to lose'* philosophy you will soon begin thinking and seeing in new ways. With Heart Dances you become a more effective part of the solutions that are so desperately needed right now. Every spiritual teaching I know of says we are capable of much more than we know.

A major benefit of working with Heart Dances is how we begin to know ourselves as eternal souls rather than mortal physical bodies. This shift from physical to soul awareness enables us to experience ourselves as the cause of our lives rather than the effect. This liberates us from reacting to and perpetuating what we don't want to create. Therefore, enabling us to create what we do want and receive what is for our Highest Good.

The 32 sacred human aspects that these Angels of the Merkabah illuminate do much more than enable us to see ourselves as the 'Light'. They enable us to *experience ourselves as the Light'* which is much more powerful. By affirming, breathing, and visualizing these internal elemental expressions of our souls light we actually facilitate clearing, balancing and liberating our soul's innate creative potential.

These holographic experiences provide dynamic personal inner journeys that open and flow through the full spectrum of human consciousness awakening and encouraging you to surf the inner realms of your own loving. Angels of the Merkabah helped us see these radiant human aspects of 'Light' and assemble them into experiences to accelerate awareness of 'The Light,' 'The Creator,' Who is Love within us all. It has been a journey beyond our wildest imaginations! We'd love to hear about your experiences and creative uses of this technology.

Both Jesus and the gods of Eden have said "we too are gods, and that we are capable of even greater things."

As our limited linear patterns of thinking are gently revealed and then dissolved with Heart Dances, your innate sacred wisdom within is illuminated. Embracing this superior wisdom of your holographic feeling heart is how to become a responsible co-creator with God. Awakened to the unconditional loving within and all around us, we will all be changed in the "Blink of an Eye."

"The 'cosmic dance' is the divine movement of our awareness from earth to heaven and back and forth. Flowing between the worlds of illusion and light without attaching or resisting anything, we become conscious participants in the assimilation and transformation of our earthly lives into heavenly ones. As we move from the outer illusion to the inner heavens, we create our own bridge. Over this bridge, God's love flows through us and into our lives."

Quote by Bodie McCoy from his book 'The Eighth Heaven"

As in this design, every person, like each dot, holds a unique position in the greater whole. We are all integral parts of the perfection of the universe. As each of us awakens to this perfection, we begin to honor our lives as the gift it is, and it truly becomes magical!

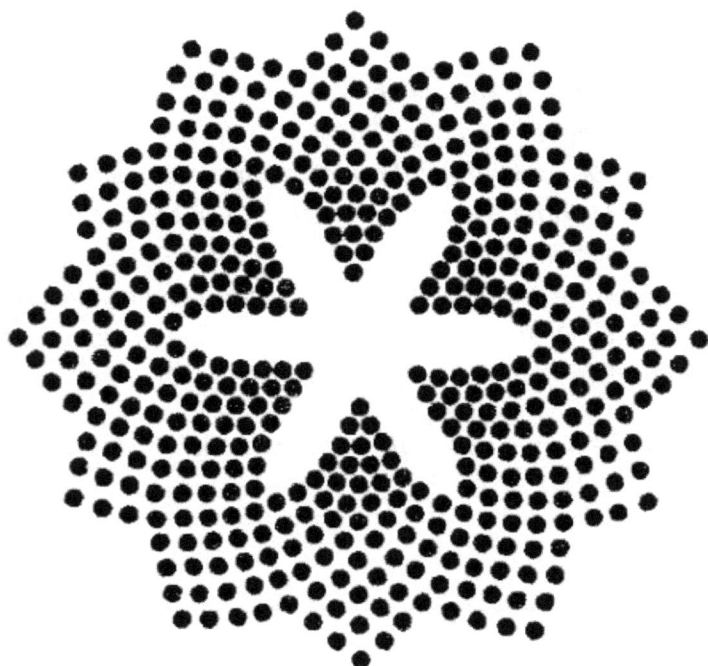

www.ingramcontent.com/pod-product-compliance
Lightning Source LLC
Chambersburg PA
CBHW072046080426
42733CB00010B/2013